TAKE MORE NAPS

(AND 100 OTHER LIFE LESSONS)

By Dr. Keen Babbage

INTERNATIONAL
RRP
PUBLISHING

RRP International Publishing LLC
Richmond/Lexington, Ky.

RRP International LLC, DBA Eugenia Ruth LLC
330 Eastern Bypass
Ste #1 Box 302
Richmond, Ky. 40475

www.rrpinternational.org

ISBN-13: 978-0-9793644-3-3

Previous Books:

The Art of Opinion Writing: Insider Secrets from Top Op-Ed Columnists

The Art of Column Writing: Insider Secrets from Art Buchwald, Dave Barry, Arianna Huffington, Pete Hamill and Other Great Columnists

Don McNay's Greatest Hits: Ten Years as an Award-Winning Columnist

Life Lessons from Cancer

Son of a Son of a Gambler: Joe McNay 80th Birthday Edition

Life Lessons from the Golf Course: The Quest for Spiritual Meaning, Psychological Understanding and Inner Peace through the Game of Golf

Life Lessons from the Lottery: Protecting Your Money in a Scary World

Wealth Without Wall Street: A Main Street Guide to Making Money

Son of a Son of a Gambler: Winners, Losers and What to Do When You Win the Lottery

DEDICATION

To Dr. Adron Doran and Mrs. Mignon Doran

TABLE OF CONTENTS

PREFACE

Naps are for infants, toddlers and children. I learned in my mid-40s that naps are also for adults.

What changed? I started wearing reading glasses at age 41, right on schedule my eye doctor consoled me. Reading glasses were for old people. I needed reading glasses. Age was demanding more attention from me and new concessions from me.

The next impact of age was noticed in running. My hometown hosts a July 4th 10K run annually and I almost always participate. During my 40s I continued to participate, yet my finishing time kept getting slower year after year. It was little consolation that I could see the finish line time clock without using my reading glasses.

The next signal was aches and pains that were associated with no injury; rather, they were associated with 45 or 50 years of living. Someone told me that after gravity tugs at you for 50 years there can be some pain. Is that diagnosis accurate?

The final signal that life was changing came one weekend afternoon when, after grading some papers or planning some lessons for my classes, I would lie down on the bed. I intended to stay there only a few minutes to rest. That short rest soon became a nap, which, much to my delight, was healing, refreshing and invigorating.

The conclusion was quite certain–take more naps. This thought led to several, actually many, years of reflection. Was there anything else in life that I should do more of? Was there anything else in life that I should do less of? This book presents those reflections.

Thank you for reading *Take More Naps*. I hope the book is encouraging, instructional and provocative for you. I also hope that you will occasionally pause in your reading and go do what the pages are encouraging you to do. So, please read more pages, think more thoughts, touch more lives, and take more naps.

These 101 essays were written during a collection of years as I moved from my 40s to 50s. As you journey through these essays, know that there have been many moments which have been reflected on throughout the years. The lessons learned from these moments and from these years can apply to people of all ages, living in any time period. Naps are universal and are forever good. I trust that the ideas in this book are equally beneficial and applicable.

Some of the essays build upon very exact, personal experiences. Other essays have a more general foundation. Some essays offer a very direct insight and action. Other essays require more reflection to discover the insights and subsequent applications.

Some essays refer to my dear mother and my dear father. Mom died in 2010. Dad died in 2001. They both lived honorable, exemplary, meaningful lives which continue to inspire many people, including me.

Some essays refer to various jobs I have had. I have been very fortunate to have had work experiences which created opportunities to achieve and to learn.

I encourage the reader to pause often while reading these essays. Read an essay, think about the essay, go do something good that the essay reminded, inspired or provoked you to do. Read another essay and repeat the process. Then take a nap, read and take an action.

I had to take one long pause while working on this book. The pause was during 2010-2013 because in October 2010 I was diagnosed with sinus cancer. This type of cancer was rare, aggressive and potentially deadly. Faith, family and friends have enabled me to defeat cancer so far. Cancer never gives up, so the war continues in various ways.

During the years that I have been in a war with cancer, many prayers have been prayed, many treatments have been endured, many very helpful medical professionals have been seen, many days of school had to be missed, my family members have been angels, friends have been supportive and many naps have been taken.

Following surgeries in June 2012 and June 2013, my body insisted on more naps. Some of those naps were for two or three hours, but that was only for a few weeks. Still, taking more naps was necessary and beneficial. I listened to my body and to the title of this book.

Please note the ideas in this book are not based on statistics, research or science. The ideas in this book come from life experiences. This book is filled with life lessons, including take more naps.

Keen Babbage, Ed. D.
Lexington, Kentucky
September 2014

1. TAKE MORE NAPS

Sunday afternoon about 2:30, after lunch is finished, after the newspaper has been read, after church has been attended, after all plans for the rest of the day for everyone in the family have been agreed to–after these or other Sunday endeavors have been completed, the perfect way to spend the next hour is to take a nap. Naps made sense when we were children. Naps still make sense. We remove naps from our routine not because they have lost their beneficial powers, but more likely because the rapid overscheduled pace of life says that time for a nap just cannot be found in an already overcrowded day. Sunday is designed to be a day of rest, so at least a nap can be included.

If we have seven hours of tasks to do on a Sunday from 2:30 to 9:30, what happens if we take a nap from 2:30 to 3:30 and then do our tasks from 3:30 to 9:30? We would probably get seven hours of activities done in six hours because our heart, mind, body and soul would function better than if we had been active relentlessly, but napless.

Notice the idea in the verb used when we say "take a nap". It's as if a gift is being offered and all that is required is for the gift to be taken. Why reject such a wonderful, free, healthy, simple gift?

Take more naps. Is it possible that taking more naps could make a difference in how we feel, in how we work, in how we treat other people, in how clearly we think and in how optimistically we encounter parts of life? The result from my non-scientific experiment is that I always feel better after a nap than before a nap. There are still bills to pay and there is still work to do. There are still chores to complete and problems to solve. It's just that after a nap it seems that doing all of that is less difficult and more manageable.

Take more naps. Children who are overdue for a nap can get irritable and moody and disagreeable. Maybe adults are more similar to children than we believe.

Take more naps. That idea is actually bigger than just allocating an hour on Saturday or Sunday afternoons for some extra sleep. Take more naps includes the idea that it is good to slow down more often than we speed up. It can be a good idea to sit down for a meal instead of eating on the run. It can be good to watch the sunset instead of watching another television program.

"Take more naps. Who are you kidding? There's no time for a nap. I'm on the go all the time. I can't get everything done as it is. How can I take one hour out of my hectic schedule and sleep?"

Exactly. It is because of that hectic schedule that a nap is necessary. It is because you have too much to do that you need a nap or 30 minutes sitting silently as you read a book or 30 minutes listening to tranquil music or 30 minutes of just sitting. If it is the nap that seems awkward, slow down in a different way, but do slow down.

"I'm moving too fast to slow down." Exactly. Speed of living is not the ultimate measure of how well a life is lived. Faster living does not assure better living. Slow down. Take a deep breath. Take more naps.

As a child and as a teenager, I had a severe speech impediment. Years of speech therapy helped reduce the problem, but not completely remove the problem. Finally, during high school, the problem was solved when a high school senior took the time to ask me, a lowly high school sophomore, to be on the speech team. The senior had never heard me speak, but was being friendly since he knew my family. He took the time; he slowed down for a minute to talk to me. It's really good sometimes to slow down.

From that point on my speaking moved toward and soon arrived at, normal. Why? I had to do well for a person who took the time and made the effort to care about me.

Take more naps. Slow down. Of course, we can't nap all day every day. We cannot slow down to the pace of lethargy. Somewhere between living at burn out speed and living at super slow motion, is a reasonable pace. Taking more naps can help get us to that reasonable pace.

2. TAKE SMALLER STEPS

"I'll never lose that much weight–47 pounds. There's no way. Maybe 10 pounds or even 20, but 47 pounds just cannot happen."

"Run 26 miles? Impossible. Sure I run and I stay in good shape, but I can't run a marathon. Five or six miles, sure, but never 26 miles."

"Start dating again, at my age? Come on. I never thought I'd be single at age 44. Where would I go to meet anyone?"

"Save money for retirement? With all of our bills, we can't make ends meet now. There's no money left over for saving."

"I know my grades are not great, but I never make an F. What's wrong if I just pass every class? Other people make the Honor Roll. How could I get my C average up to the Honor Roll level? Come on, I'm a 'C' student and that's just the way it is."

Lose weight one pound at a time. One glass of water instead of one sugared soft drink at a time. One "no thank you" to dessert at a time. One smaller portion of food at a time. One movie without concession stand snacks at a time. One extra bit of exercise at a time. People do not lose 47 pounds. People lose one pound, then another pound, then 45 more pounds, one at a time.

Running a marathon requires months and months of preparation with gradual increases in the distances you run week after week. Some running experts suggest no more than a 10 percent increase in miles per week. Run five miles one week, perhaps spread out over three separate runs. Run 5.5 miles the next week, again divided over three separate runs. These two weeks may follow a few weeks of walking, jogging, walking until the endurance grows. How will this get you to the 26 miles of a marathon? Let's look…

Week 1	Walk 6 miles
Week 2	Walk/jog 6 miles
Week 3	Jog 6 miles
Week 4	jog 6.6 miles
Week 5	jog/run 7.3 miles
Week 6	jog/run 8.0 miles
Week 7	jog/run 8.8 miles
Week 8	jog/run 9.7 miles
Week 9	jog/run 10.7 miles
Week 10	jog/run 11.8 miles
Week 11	jog/run 13.0 miles
Week 12	jog/run 14.3 miles
Week 13	run 15.7 miles
Week 14	run 17.3 miles
Week 15	run 19.0 miles
Week 16	run 20.9 miles
Week 17	run 23 miles
Week 18	run 25.3 miles
Week 19	run 27.8 miles
Week 20	run 30.6 miles
Week 21	run 33.7 miles
Week 22	run 37.2 miles
Week 23	run 40.8 miles
Week 24	run 44.9 miles
Week 25	run 49.4 miles
Week 26	run 54.3 miles

After about six months of running, you are ready for a marathon even though six months earlier it was challenging to walk two miles. What is similar about the two mile walk and the 26-mile marathon run? Each is done one step at a time!

How does a person who is unexpectedly single at age 44 start dating? Go where other people who are 44, single and compatible with you are. Go to a single's Bible Study Class at church. Help build a Habitat for Humanity house that a young adult group is working on. Volunteer with community groups. Join a tennis club or a fitness club. Go to PTA meetings. Play on an over-40 soccer team.

Ask friends to introduce you to friends. The bottom line is to be active–your next date will not magically knock on your door.

How do you save money for retirement? One dollar at a time. Save $1.00 daily and you have $365 per year. Just give up a cup of coffee or a soft drink daily and the $1.00 or more daily is yours. Spend less–save more. It is OK to not spend money.

Ideally, the first check each month is written to your savings account. This is not the last payment with what's left over after necessities are paid for and after optional items are paid for.

Save $8.00 per day starting at age 22 and invest this in your Individual Retirement Account. Do this for 40 years making adjustments as income increases and as the IRA maximum annual contribution goes up. Invest it cautiously. Result? At age 62 you win big because you saved $8.00 per day, one day at a time.

How does a student get better grades? One homework assignment at a time. Always do the homework on time, completely and correctly, for all classes. Be on time to class, pay attention, do the work, listen, answer questions, ask questions. Read. Read more. Keep reading. Turn off the television, turn off the video games and turn off the social media. Use all the brain power you have instead of using all the excuses you can imagine.

The take more naps idea and the take smaller steps idea fit together perfectly. There are more ideas which also fit with these. Let's read them one idea at a time, one page at a time. Then after reading a few pages and thinking a few thoughts, a short nap would be perfect.

3. THINK BETTER THOUGHTS

"Let's go see a different movie. That one you mentioned has such awful violence in it and much crude language. I really don't want those pictures or words to be stuck in my mind. Once they get in my brain, there is no way to delete them."

"Do I really want to read that book? Yeah, it sold a lot of copies, but I heard people say, well, that the story was all about terrible things that some awful criminal did. I guess people get interested in that stuff, but I just don't like to think about mass murder or serial killers."

"Come on, let's check out that website everybody was talking about. Can you believe those pictures are on the internet? Nobody will ever know what we looked at. It'll be fun. Come on. What's wrong? You got something better to do?"

The answer is yes. There is much to do that is better. Why is it so important to think better thoughts, to think the best possible thoughts, to put into our brain the best possible content? One reason is that the human brain does not delete. Pictures, images, graphics, lyrics, words and ideas which we allow into our brain cannot be erased. The brain does not have a delete key, an undo key or an escape key.

Another reason is that while not all thoughts lead to action, all actions come after and come as a result of a thought. A person realizes that she is thirsty and thinks, "Water would be good. I need to drink more water. So, water it is." The person did not have to think to become thirsty. The thirst emerged as a physical reality and the brain realized it. The thinking was about how to quench the thirst. The thinking resulted in the action to drink water and to not drink other beverages.

A person thinks about the homeless problem in his community. He wonders what he can do about this. He investigates and learns that the local Salvation Army provides some services for people in need. He thinks about this and decides to volunteer some time once a week at the Salvation Army. A different thought which would lead to a different action or inaction would be "I'm glad that's not me. I'd hate to be homeless and hungry."

Think better thoughts. What happens when you think about the word "hope"? Contrast that with what happens when you think about the words "I quit, I give up, I'm no good". Notice that heart, mind, body and/or soul really shift in feeling, comfort level, energy level, expression and more as the two different approaches to hope are heard and thought about.

Thinking is not magic. I hope, I hope, I hope, I hope that the weather is good on Friday. That adds to my optimistic anticipation of Friday, but I need to have plan B ready should Friday's weather be bad.

Thinking is not magic. I hope I make this free throw shot. If you have practiced hundreds and thousands of free throws, and done well in practice, you'll probably make the shot. If you think you'll be in a situation someday where you'll need to make a free throw, let that thought guide you to action now–lots of good free throw practice–so you'll be ready when the free throw moment of truth arrives.

Think better thoughts, such as:

- hope
- kindness
- welcome
- friend
- never give up
- sunshine
- peace
- good health
- family
- hospitality
- love
- progress
- meeting a challenge
- mastering a skill
- correcting a mistake
- forgiveness
- make amends
- compassion
- volunteering

The reader is asked to think of more good thoughts to complete the list above.

-
-
-
-
-
-
-
-

4. CORRECT MORE MISTAKES

How can a mistake which has already been made be corrected? How can the unkind word spoken yesterday be fully resolved and prevented from impacting today? How can the good book not read, the church service not attended, the sympathy card not sent, the physical exercise not attempted or the phone call not made in the past be resolved now, today, if the mistake has already been made and the damage has already been done?

First, immediately do what should have been done. The book to read can be started today and a reading schedule of pages to read per day can be put in writing and followed. If a Sunday morning church service was not attended, find a Sunday night service or a weekday service to attend. The card or letter or e-mail that should have been sent yesterday can still be sent today and can still do lots of good. If physical exercise cannot be scheduled, take the steps to help make up for the elusive workout. The phone call that was needed yesterday may be too late for a deadline or other time-specific benefits, but as a courtesy can still be made today.

Second, unlike the mistakes described above where an action not taken yesterday just needs a substitute or needs to be taken today to correct a mistake, other actions or inactions of yesterday may require more effort.

"I'm sorry. I was wrong. You played much better than I did. You deserved to win that tennis match. I'm sorry I yelled so much. I wanted to call and apologize. Hey, let's get together for lunch today, my treat."

"I told you we would go to the park yesterday and I just kept putting it off. I was wrong. Let's go right now. We'll stay as long as you want to, plus we'll get a really healthy juice drink at your favorite shop after we go to the park."

"I know it was expensive. I know we are saving for that trip. I should not have bought it. Listen, the budget we set up included $200 in clothes for me next month. I'll skip the clothes. That $200 more than makes up for what I spent today on the gardening supplies."

Third, some mistakes are not isolated events, but are repeated. A person is always late to work, to family events, to everything. A person tells crude jokes or uses vulgar language even when children are nearby. A person drives too fast, runs red lights and never stops at stop signs. A person gets more and more in debt using more and more credit cards. A person shops and shops while already having more than enough of everything.

Taking more naps will not correct these mistakes. Taking more actions will. Seeing the mistakes as mistakes is essential. "Oh, that's just the way I am," is unacceptable. Replacing the mistaken action with a proper action is next. Stop, actually halt, at the red light. Be five minutes early to everything. Eliminate credit card use that creates costly and excessive debt. Immediately pay off credit card bills if credit cards must be used.

Correcting more mistakes also has a favorable option–do not make the mistake to start with. Do not use the vulgar language to begin with. Do not drive too fast at all. Send the sympathy message right now while you are thinking about it. Perhaps prevention of mistakes is the best correction. When prevention does not happen, swift, realistic, genuine, sincere and lasting correction is necessary.

Today: I will correct a mistake I made yesterday.

The mistake was

_____

The mistake was made because

_____

I will correct the mistake today by taking this action:

_____

This Week and This Month: I will correct a mistake I keep making over and over.

The mistake was

_____

The mistake was made because

_____

I will correct the mistake this week and this month by taking these actions:

_____

I could have prevented this mistake pattern altogether if I had

_____

5. BE MORE DECISIVE

"Yes."

"No."

"Can you meet me for lunch at noon at the Main Street Cafeteria?"

"Yes, you may use the car tonight if by 6:00 p.m. you have finished all of the yard work, cleaned the garage and cleaned your room."

"No, I don't put alcohol or other drugs in my body. I think I'll just leave this place before it gets crazy here."

"The job offer is yours. Do you accept it or not? We need to know now."

"Fast ball, a little high, but not much. Do I swing at it or not?"

"On sale, three for $30, but the ones I have are still ok. I can live without those new shirts."

"I will devote myself to you. I will love you forever like no man ever loved his wife. Will you marry me?"

"It is time to go right now. We're leaving."

"Are you going to apply to that college or not? The deadline is in two weeks. You need to decide now."

How can the take more naps approach be applied to being more decisive? Well, making the decision and the commitment to take more naps is decisive. Actually carrying out the decision and the commitment is more decisive.

There is more to consider. Taking an occasional nap indicates that you are in charge of your schedule. You plan time or you make time as needed to take care of your heart, mind, body and soul. That is decisive.

What is so good about being decisive? Does decisive mean thinking fast or being slow, methodical and cautious?

Imagine an umpire at a baseball game calling balls and strikes, safe or out. Quick, precise, decisive determinations are expected from the umpire. It would be unacceptable for an umpire to say, "Pretty good pitch. It was not too high and not too low. It was coming right at the corner of home plate. I will give it some thought." Umpires are required to make instant and accurate decisions. Umpires are trained to do this decisively and quickly.

Emergency medical experts arrive on a scene where injuries need quick, accurate, effective attention. Lengthy consideration of options may not be available in a crisis; however, emergency medical experts are trained to be decisive and to take action now.

A husband may begin thinking today of the perfect birthday gift for his wife whose birthday is in one month. The decision of what gift to give is not needed now. Some time to think, to get suggestions from friends of his wife, to get hints from his wife and to shop around would make sense. Still, well before the birthday date, the husband needs to decisively select the gift, purchase the gift and wrap the gift. The husband's decision schedule was different than the schedule of the baseball umpire, but both worked for their purposes.

Be more decisive means make the right decision in the right way at the right time for the right reasons.

What happens when a person is indecisive? What happens when a person is indecisive? What happens when a person is indecisive? Get the point of no answer being given to the question "What happens when a person is indecisive?" What happened was that the same question kept getting asked with no answer, resolution, conclusion, decision or action. Decisive is about what happens. Indecisive is about what does not happen.

To be more decisive a person must establish a system for decision making. Different types of decisions may need different systems. Some decisions are made once and never need to be reconsidered. For example, it is wrong to steal, it has always been wrong to steal and it will always be wrong to steal. Stealing does not need to be reviewed. The decision is already made.

To decide which car to buy requires thorough evaluation of finances, transportation needs, performance evaluation of cars, personal priorities and marketplace realities. The car which made sense 10 years ago may or may not make sense now.

Today I need to decide

_____

The decision making process will include

_____

The benefits of deciding now are

_____

The problems of delaying a decision are

_____

Being indecisive would mean that

_____

6. BE MORE TRUSTWORTHY

"You have my word on it."

"I give you my word."

"Yes, you can trust me to be there on time."

"No, I cannot do that. If I made that compromise, how could I be trusted?"

"I really want to go to the game with you, but I promised my family I'd go to my grandfather's birthday party. I need to be there for him. Please, let's go to another game soon."

"You gave me too much change. The bill was $7.75 and I gave you $10.00, but you gave me change like I gave you $20.00. It's more important to me to be honest than to get 10 easy dollars."

"I wish I could attend the meeting, but there is another commitment that day that I need to honor. I can meet with you another day, but I can't come Wednesday. I promised to be somewhere else on Wednesday."

"We said that opening night would be Friday, April 22. This is hard work. We are behind with set construction and rehearsals, but we will open the spring musical on April 22."

"You need to be home at 10:00 tonight. I'm going to trust you to be on time. Even if other people stay later, you need to be home at 10:00 because you'll be getting up tomorrow morning for your baseball game."

"I'll get these reports finished by Monday morning. I know how important this project is. You can count on me."

"Here's a five dollar bill. The ice cream costs two dollars. I'm trusting you to bring me the three dollars in change."

Life works better when we take more naps because we restore the body. Life works better when we mean what we say and say what we mean in clear, polite, certain, decisive terms. Life also works better when we keep our word, make proper promises and keep them, make proper commitments and keep them, honor obligations even when new opportunities arise that cause a conflict and when we live up to the proper trust that people place in us.

How is trustworthiness earned and learned? Day by day in small steps at first. A child understands that all toys have to be put back in their proper place. Any toy left out is taken away for a week.

A child is given clean-up duties and other chores at home as conditions for receiving a weekly allowance. A teenager commits to earning good grades, to doing volunteer work in the community, to reaching a certain goal in Scouts, or in karate, or in playing a musical instrument. A young adult earns the opportunity to use the family car after certain requirements are met and can keep using the car on an agreed to schedule if further requirements are honored.

How do parents and guardians build trust from their children? Among the many ways is to be there, be there, and be there. When a child sees, feels, hears your loving presence, life makes a lot more sense for the child and the child can see the importance of, plus the actions of, being trustworthy from your example.

How does a high school theater director help the cast and crew make up for lost time? An exact schedule is agreed to. Commitments are confirmed. Progess is celebrated.

Being more trustworthy means that today I need to

_____

_____

7. BE MORE THRIFTY

Save, save more, keep saving. Save, save more, keep saving. Save, save more, keep saving. Have you memorized those words yet? Living by those words can help make financial success much more possible.

Save. Put your pocket change in a container daily and save it for a year. Put one dollar away daily and when the holiday shopping season arrives, you have your shopping fund. Say no to one cup of coffee or soft drink each day for a year and the saving is hundreds of dollars or more. Imagine a student in the 6th grade who does not buy a $1 soft drink each day after school for a year, but who saves $1 daily. When the school year ends, the student has saved $175. If the same student did that during 6th grade through 12th grade, the savings reach $1,225.

Save more. Know the prices of products so when you see a store reduce laundry detergent from $8.98 to $7.98 and will double your 50 cent coupon so the cost is $6.98, you already know that another store sells the same product at an everyday price of $7.12, so use the non-doubled coupon at the everyday low price store and you pay $6.62.

Look for alternatives. Sure it is enjoyable to visit an amusement park, but if it costs $30 or $40 or more per person just to get in, that adds up. Ten dollars can be saved on admission with a coupon from the nearby grocery store, so get some coupons. The children in the family can earn some money to help pay for the amusement park trip to add a vital economics lesson.

Of course, it is not necessary to go to the amusement park at all. There could be a wonderful family day of games, activities, a cook out, cookies to bake and new traditions to start with new memories created. All of that costs much less than the trip to the amusement park and all of that could be more meaningful for the family. Sure, an occasional trip to the costly amusement park may fit in the budget, but there are other options that save money and provide as much or more delight.

Keep saving. Part of the beauty and part of the power of capitalism is competition. Keep saving by taking full advantage of capitalism. One office supply store features a paper folder with two pockets and three clips to hold notebook paper for 15 cents each. They have a sale with buy one, get one free, so two cost 15 cents A nearby store lowers their price to seven cents and then to five cents. Why go from seven cents to five cents? Because a third store charged six cents. Of course, don't spend endless hours and endless gallons of gas to save one cent, but do take advantage of competition whenever possible.

Another effective way to keep saving is to not spend. Breathing and a pulse are essential to life. Going out to supper is not essential to life. Going out to movies is not essential to life. Fixing a meal at home is efficient and inexpensive. Reading a good book that is already on your shelf at home is a great alternative to a night at the movies. Of course, meals at a restaurant might fit in the budget, especially if it is a moderately priced restaurant. Going to the movies could fit in the budget, especially if it is the bargain movie theater or the lower priced early afternoon showing. Still, it is quite possible to save lots of money, have very good meals and enjoy pleasant evenings at home with family members and friends.

Let's do the math. A person has a job where it works perfectly to take a brown bag lunch to work. The food taken in the brown bag lunch costs $1.50 and could be healthy, tasty and enjoyable. Going out to lunch could easily cost $5 to $10, so use $7.50 as the average. The brown bag option done four days a week, not all five work days, saves $24 per week or about $100 per month. That is real money which could more than pay for an annual trip to the amusement park with money left over for the savings account.

I can save money in these ways:

Today: _____

This week: _____

This month: _____

This year_____

8. HAVE A TO NOT DO LIST

It is very common to use a "to do" list daily. This list might be written on an index card, on a page in a weekly/monthly planner or on another time management system. The list could be entered in an electronic scheduling device or program. A "to do" list can be a very effective way to manage time, to get results, to increase efficiency, to avoid "Oh, I forgot to do that" and to assist in the minute to minute, day to day duties of life.

It is uncommon to use a "to not do" list, but this type of list could have vast benefits. The "to not do" list may or may not need to be on paper or on the electronic screen, but it needs to be taken just as seriously even if memory and habit are the methods used instead of paper or screen. Note: Split infinitive purists will prefer "not to do" versus "to not do". Your choice.

Possible items for a "to not do" list could include these:
- Do not lie
- Do not cheat
- Do not steal
- Do not overeat
- Do not waste time
- Do not watch endless television
- Do not waste money
- Do not procrastinate
- Do not leave home without saying "I love you" to each family member
- Do not fight
- Do not argue about unimportant topics
- Do not surf the internet endlessly or do social media endlessly
- Do not eat so much junk food
- Do not skip exercising
- Do not make excuses
- Do not be late

- Do not talk on the phone, drink, eat, groom or text while driving
- Do not run stop signs
- Do not run red lights
- Do not turn a car without signaling
- Do not stay up too late
- Do not blame someone else when it is your fault
- Do not expect children to follow a standard you will not follow
- Do not say hurtful words
- Do not complain about some condition without being willing to actually do something about it
- Do not speak as much or more than you listen
- Do not judge something or someone you know nothing about
- Do not violate laws
- Do not say to a child "we'll do that later" and risk losing the moment now when doing it right now is possible
- Do not over schedule with more than can be done well in a day
- Do not delay medical check-ups and procedures that could detect problems early or prevent problems altogether
- Do not skip breakfast
- Do not yell at the ball in golf, soccer, tennis, basketball or any other sport
- Do not hit, kick or throw the ball the same way you did when it did not work the way you wanted it to
- Do not ignore good advice
- Do not stay in the wrong job too long or leave a good job too soon
- Do not put yourself or your family in financial risk
- Do not hit the snooze button on the alarm clock.

Removing the causes of failure can help increase the possibility of success. With that in mind, create some "To not do" lists of your own, for today, this week and this year.

9. BE MORE INVOLVED

- Red Cross
- Salvation Army
- Homeless Shelter
- School fund raising project
- Parent Teacher Association (PTA)
- Church
- Food bank
- Big Brothers/Big Sisters
- March of Dimes
- Local 5K race
- The local 4th of July parade
- Thanksgiving food basket programs
- Canned food drive
- Special Olympics
- Sunday School
- Meals on Wheels
- Youth soccer, baseball, basketball or other activities
- Nursing home
- Hospital
- Blood bank
- Humane society
- Charity fund raising events
- Cancer society
- Leukemia society marathons
- Local golf, tennis, swimming events
- Charity auctions
- Radio reading services for blind people or visually impaired people
- Community clean-up project
- High school marching band equipment manager
- Telethons
- Political campaigns
- City council meetings

- School board meetings
- YMCA or YWCA
- Boys Club or Girls Club
- Senior Citizens Centers

The list could be much longer, but the idea remains the same. Select one or two ways to be more involved in your community, find out how to be more involved and then do it.

The idea is not to make your already impossibly busy schedule busier, but to rethink the priorities. Maybe two hours per week of television time could become two hours per week of reading a good book to residents of a nursing home. If you lived in a nursing home, you would appreciate people coming to read good books to you.

Families can volunteer together. Imagine the lessons learned by children when Thanksgiving Day includes the entire family spending time to help serve a holiday meal at a local homeless center.

Take a minute and list some very interesting and very feasible involvement activities you could consider in your community:

-
-
-
-
-
-
-
-

Now select two items from the list and get involved.

Item 1:_____and to get involved in this, I

will_____

Item 2:_____and to get involved in this, I

will_____

10. VISIT NURSING HOMES

One example of getting more involved is to visit nursing homes. Please read the following paragraphs to get an idea of what a visit like that could mean.

"Hi, Ruth, we came to visit again. How have you been?" Kim Pauling walked into Ruth Vaughn's room in the Coventry Nursing Home. Kim's 12-year-old daughter, Marti, came along. Ruth was sitting up in bed, but obviously was not having a very good day. She managed to smile and to speak softly. "Oh, dear, Kim, I'm so glad you are here. It's been so long and who is that pretty young girl with you?"

Marti smiled, but also looked a bit confused. She wondered silently, doesn't Ms. Ruth remember me? We were here last week. That's not so long, but it was to Ms. Ruth.

Kim answered, "Well, Ruth, you remember Marti. She's my oldest child. Her younger, twin brothers are at a camp this week. It has been a while since we were here. A week or so, I think, but it's so good to be here today."

Ruth answered after coughing a few times and clearing her throat. "Marti, could you come hand me that glass of water. I guess I could reach it, but since you are here, I'll ask for your help."

Marti was glad to hand Ruth the water, but she did wonder what Ruth would have done about the water if she and her mother had not come today.

"Ruth, Marti and I brought a story to read to you. Actually, Marti wrote the story for her project at school last year. She's rewritten it a few times and we think you would like it."

"Oh, that is just perfect. I'll listen to every word." Ruth and Kim traded smiles as Marti started reading. The story finished with this conclusion.

"So, it was the best birthday party ever. All of my best friends were there. We played games. We played our favorite music. We had tons of cake and ice cream. We opened presents."

"Then a big, long, white limousine stopped in front of my house. I knew nothing about it, but everyone else knew. All of my friends, my parents, and my brothers got in the limousine and we went to the skateboard park. I got to use my brand new skateboard which was a present I had just opened at my party. It was the best birthday party ever."

Marti had brought the skateboard to show Ruth what it was in case she had never seen a skateboard. Ruth amazed Marti by saying, "My grandson, Josh, has one of those. He's told me all about the skateboard park. Maybe I'll get to go there someday."

Marti looked at her mother and Mom nodded her head yes. Mrs. Pauling said, "Well, Ruth, let's just get your grandson and Marti to join us next week for a trip to the skateboard park. Do you think you'll feel well enough to go?"

Ruth paused and then said almost loudly, "Nothing could stop me."

For Kim and Marti the visit to the nursing home was an opportunity to do something good for Ruth.

For Ruth the visit gave a reason to look forward to a big event the next week.

The visit cost no money, but required some time and some compassion. The rewards of the visit cannot be measured but truly are priceless and endless.

11. CHERISH MORE MEMORIES

"What was it like before television? What did everybody do?" A curious child asks her grandfather.

"What do you mean no computers? How did anything work?" asks the technology savvy teenager of his grandmother.

"You played baseball when you were little, but the field is not there anymore. What happened?" the 10-year-old little league first baseman asked his father.

"Was grandma a soccer mom for you like you are for me or did they have soccer moms back then?" the inquisitive 11-year-old daughter asks her mother.

"Where did you go to school? Is the building still there? Did you go to school with anybody famous?" asks the fifth grader of his teacher.

"What was Christmas like when you were my age? What did you do?" the eight-year-old great granddaughter wants to know from her great grandmother.

Memories can be shared, recorded, kept alive and cherished. Sure, some memories are sad or painful, frightening or disturbing. Still, the charming and cherished memories of family members, of life in earlier generations, of childhood, of friendships, of school, of growing up, of graduation, a first job, a goal reached, an honor earned, a mission accomplished, a worthy sacrifice completed or a challenge overcome merit reflections, retelling, being handed down and being written down.

Imagine that an older family member is sick and during recuperation needs help. Hospital or nursing home care really are more than is needed, but for a few weeks this distinguished senior citizen cannot live alone despite an insistence on independence.

Of course, arrangements are made for Grandpa to live with his son, his daughter-in-law and his two grandchildren. This is the right action to take. Will it be an awkward, inconvenient imposition or will it be a remarkable, inspiring adventure of time together that will include sharing memories of years past and creating memories for years and for generations to come? Imagine the long conversations, almost like oral history, that Grandpa and the grandchildren could share. "Mom, Dad, did you know that Grandpa flew a plane in the Army Air Corps? Can you believe that? Wait 'til I tell everyone at school that my grandpa won the war."

Cherishing more memories means giving memories some time, effort and reflection. Gather the family, create a list of topics and begin the audio and/or video recording. Go through the family archives, souvenirs, and treasures from the attic, basement, closets and drawers to see what stories go with the items. "Who is in this picture with Mom? Is that you, Dad, is that really you?" Scrap books can be a wonderful way to cherish memories and to preserve memories.

Think of memories you would like to cherish and of actions you could take to preserve those memories.

Memories to Cherish

How to Preserve Those Memories

12. FOLLOW WISE ADVICE

"Put a dime in a jar today. Then tomorrow, put another dime in the same jar. Do that every day. Then one of these days when you need new tires for your car, you'll have the money saved up."

My grandfather gave me that advice in 1968. I was 14 years old. He was 72 years old. His advice was wise. No doubt, the daily amount of saving needs to be increased to adjust for inflation, but the wisdom endures.

"Life gets more complicated." I heard those words in 1978 while eating lunch with a colleague in the company cafeteria at the large corporation where I worked. My friend was speaking of his children, their orthodontist bills, their college education costs, their schedules and the demands of mom, dad, wife, husband and family. He cherished his family. He had goals for his career. He spoke as a wise 40-something, mature adult to a 20-something maturing adult. I saw few complexities in life at age 24, but in the 30 plus years that have passed since that advice was given, I have seen the complexities grow and grow.

"People support what they help create", said Dr. Earl Reum at a leadership conference in July 1971 at Georgetown College in Georgetown, Kentucky. About 200 high school students attended the conference. Dr. Reum spoke many wise words throughout many decades to hundreds of thousands of teenage leaders throughout this nation.

"Love you lots." Perhaps that statement does not appear to be advice, but it does work as wisdom. In July 2001, my father became very ill. For eight months he had lived in hospitals and nursing homes, but it was now obvious that his poor health was declining rapidly.

Two days before his peaceful death, Dad and I shared our final conversation. He had very little to say, but he smiled occasionally and he looked quite deeply into my eyes, into my heart and into my soul. When it was time for me to leave the hospital, I held Dad's hand and said to him, "Dad, I love you a lot." He used his remaining strength to lovingly squeeze my hand, to smile, to direct his total attention to me and say, "Love you lots". Those were the last words my dear father spoke aloud to me, but I hear those precious words daily.

"Love you lots." To live a life of loving lots of people with lots of love, that's what Dad advises me to do daily. Wise advice from a wonderful father whom I will forever love lots.

My mother's words to our family as she neared death in 2010 were, "If I die, do not grieve. Rejoice that I lived a good life." Wisdom. Part of her good life was that she loved lots of people and loved them a lot.

People to whom I need to say "Love you lots" to today:

Name   When, Where, How I will say it

13. BUILD MORE BRIDGES

Interactive. Interdependent. The human brain is organized for making connections between what is known and what is new. A child who is interested in basketball can understand math better when asked questions such as "how many points do you have if you hit 12 two point shots plus 3 three-point shots" than if asked "what is 12 times 2 and 3 times 3 added together." A person who cooks well can understand the importance of planning a meal and could offer ideas to a charity which would like to host a banquet, but cannot afford a caterer.

The amount of engineering design work which goes into the concept of and the drawing of a proposed bridge over a river is detailed with scientific and mathematical precision. The design must be flawless and must be meticulous. The actual construction of the bridge is equally demanding in precision and in attention to detail. The bridge is designed and is built through careful planning and through high quality hard work.

Apply that to the need for people to build bridges between people. We make better mental connections when new information links to something we already know, are interested in or are talented in. The brain knows how to process, use, organize and make sense out of information that connects with its current content. Perhaps some human bridges can benefit from associations that build upon similarities. People who like to play tennis can join existing tennis leagues or clubs to make instant connections with, to build quick and purposeful bridges with, other tennis players. People who share a religious faith can team up with each other to form human bridges based on spiritual bonds.

What happens when bridges need to be built between two people or two groups of people who are not as instantly harmonious as the tennis players or the religious community? Can a bridge still be built?

Consider the wisdom of Thomas Jefferson as he expressed these profound ideas in The Declaration of Independence: "We hold these truths to be self-evident, that all men are created equal, that they are endowed by their Creator with certain unalienable rights, that among these are life, liberty, and the pursuit of happiness." Those words indicate the common human rights of "life, liberty and the pursuit of happiness" and the need to bridge the span between Jefferson's ideal and life's reality.

Can labor and management find common ground which leads to symbiotic decisions? Can Republicans and Democrats find common ground which leads to symbiotic or, at least, productive decisions? Can husband and wife, brother and sister, parent and child, employer and employee, teacher and student find common ground from which they can build bridges which increase symbiotic results and which enhance meaningful, beneficial and wholesome interaction and interdependence? Yes.

How does a child build a bridge which takes her to a college education? How does a young man build a bridge which takes him to hearing "yes" when he proposes marriage to the woman he loves? How do parents build bridges which take their child from completely dependent infant to fully competent adult? How does a company build bridges with satisfied customers who return often? How does a political leader build bridges with constituents? How do concerned citizens build bridges with organizations or individuals who need help?

Pick up the phone and call, send an e-mail, write a letter, show up, be there, help out, take the initiative. If enough human bridges are built, then everyone is connected. Globally, that is an immense task. In a community, in a school, in a company, in a family, in a friendship that is a very real possibility, a very feasible task, a very vital bridge.

With whom do I need to build a bridge now?

_____

I will build this bridge by doing

_____
_____

14. SPEAK MORE SELECTIVELY

Not everything that enters the brain should come out of the mouth. "But it just slipped out. I did not mean to say it." Nonsense. Do not lie to yourself like that. The mouth speaks when the brain tells it to speak. The mouth is silent when the brain tells it to be silent.

Any word spoken by the human being is spoken intentionally. Some words are spoken wisely and other words are spoken unwisely. Some words are spoken kindly and other words are spoken unkindly. Some words are spoken to encourage and other words are spoken to destroy. Some words are spoken politely and other words are spoken impolitely. All words, even those which a person later regrets saying, are spoken intentionally. The brain can move faster than the mouth so careful editing of what is about to be said is possible.

Get in your brain a mental picture of a place which is very far from where you are now. Maybe it is a place you visited or a place you have seen a picture of, but be sure that it is a place very far from where you are now. Your brain created that mental picture instantly. The brain moves at the speed of thought. The mouth moves at the speed of speech. The brain's speed is faster than the speed of the mouth; therefore, the human being has the ability to speak selectively.

"I hate you."

"One more step and you'll regret it."

"Make me."

"Nobody will find out."

"My fault? You always start stuff. You never listen. You never talk to me."

"I don't care."

"That's not fair."

"You always believe everything she says. You never believe me."

"Well, I heard that she broke up with him, but came back and then he broke up with her and now it's just a big mess."

"So you hate school do you? Well, maybe school hates you, too."

"I don't know why I married you."

"I heard what you said about me. Don't deny it. Everyone told me. You better watch your back."

"Hey, umpire. You stink. You're awful. You should quit."

There are moments when silence is the best option. There are moments when extra thought should come before any spoken thoughts. There are moments when a facial expression can do our speaking for us. With a few seconds of thinking perhaps "We've got to work on these problems" could be said instead of "I don't know why I married you." Perhaps "It makes me so mad and frustrated when you never call if you are going to be late" could replace "I hate you." With a moment of thought "Yeah, I know what you mean, but there must be something you like about school. Tell me one thing you like at school." could replace, "So you hate school do you? Well, maybe school hates you too."

Words spoken cannot be erased or deleted. Words spoken can be chosen selectively to cause good results and to prevent bad results. Speak selectively knowing the power of the spoken word and knowing that not every word which enters the brain should exit the mouth.

Today I will speak more selectively when I talk to

_____

about _____

To do this, I will _____ and I will

not_____

15. CREATE MENTAL ADVANTAGES

"That idea came from your uncle. Don't you still have that letter he sent you about competing in sports? You know, it had ideas he got from his father, your grandpa. You should read that." Mom suggested.

"Oh, yeah. I remember that. Maybe I should read it again. I know I kept it. It's in that book, you know, the tennis book Uncle Mike gave me. I know exactly where it is."

"Dear Jason,

"Hi. The enclosed newspaper story about a recent tennis tournament may be of interest to you. Notice that in the final set one player was winning 4-1, but soon the set was 4-3. In the 8th game of that set a line judge ruled that a ball was in, but the player who was ahead 4-3 argued and yelled. You can imagine what happened next. 4-3 became 4-4 because arguing and yelling take your mind off tennis and just let the other player get the advantage. Soon the player who had been losing 4-1, maybe 1-4 is more accurate, won the match 6-4.

"That article reminded me of our recent conversation about Grandpa–my father, your grandfather. As you know, Grandpa was quite an athlete. He ran track at the University of Tennessee prior to his service in World War II, he played golf all his life, he played tennis, he swam, he played racquetball and much more.

"Even when Grandpa played against people who were younger or who were more skilled, he usually won. He may not have been the superior athlete, but he played better. His opponent may have had better skills or better physical fitness, but Grandpa played smarter and more efficiently. He did that in many sports and often baffled younger competitors.

"Of the many advantages Dad gave himself were these two: (1) he never lost self- control. He may miss a shot or he may make a mistake, but he never yelled at the ball or threw a racket or broke a golf club. He just thought about what had been done incorrectly, decided what needed to be done correctly and then did it. (2) He studied the sports so he had the mental advantages of self- control plus superior knowledge. He read books. He watched matches and analyzed what he saw.

"He knew that someone else may have physical strength or skills he did not have, but there was no reason for anyone to ever have a mental advantage over him. By mental advantage he meant that he could know more about the game than other people knew if he studied enough and he could always keep his mental control so he concentrated fully on his next shot and wasted no time or energy or concentration on anger or comments about the last shot.

"So as you drill and practice, as you train and learn, as you participate in matches and in tournaments, work harder and smarter than you ever have, work harder and smarter than anyone else, but know that even if someone else has skills or experience or speed or size or strength which seem to be superior, you can always be the best in the categories that make up mental advantage–know the game better and manage/control yourself better."

16. VISIT ANTIQUE SHOPS

At most antique shops there is no admission price, there is a tranquil atmosphere, there is ample room to wander, there is no hurry, there are endless stories to imagine about the history of the antiques and there is no requirement to buy anything.

My experience at antique shops is that people who work there are usually quite cordial, friendly, conversational, helpful and polite. Sure, they would like to sell their items, but they also would like to visit with you. Going to an antique shop is done at a saunter pace. This is not shopping done at the speed of mall merchants or scanning bar codes at self-service hurry-up automatic scan machines which grocery stores use for efficiency. "Hey, let's run in the antique shop for three minutes and buy an old desk from a one room school house" makes no sense. "Hey, let's go to the store for milk and bread. It will just take a minute." That is fine for milk and bread, but antique shops work differently.

At the antique shop you often get to ask the question "What is that?" An old piece of furniture, an old kitchen device, some ancient style of clothing or an old toy could inspire many guesses about what the item was, how it worked, who used it and what life was like when that item was state of the art.

Antique shops may have some items which were handcrafted by masters of their trade. Children who wonder what life was like when their grandparents or great-grandparents were young can get clues about that at an antique shop. Furniture, made by hand, could tell stories about great-grandmother's and great-grandfather's life on the farm decades ago.

Slow. Slower. When you go to the antique shop, move slowly. Do not have a rushed schedule that says in 25 minutes you must leave. Antique shops are trips to the past and cannot be fully appreciated if completed at the speed of typical life today.

At the antique shop you may see some items that are not antiques. You may see some items that are broken. You may see some items that are junk that did not sell at a garage sale. Those exceptions are not the parts which define the whole.

At the antique shop there will be a price for each item, but you may offer a lower price. See what happens. Amaze children who never knew that negotiating at a store is allowed.

Some towns and villages are well known for their antique shops. Park your car and walk to several shops. There might be an antique shop section of a town which includes a walking tour past historical places and historical markers. Go slowly and savor the moments.

Of all the joys that antique shop visits can bring, one of the most wonderful is that it can be a calm, tranquil, pleasant, low technology, visit through time. It's almost as if you get the benefits of taking a nap while still being awake.

17. RUN MORE MILES

Walk if you prefer. Swim if you prefer that. Treadmill, rowing machine, bicycle, elliptical trainer, aerobic exercise class, tennis, volleyball, basketball, square dancing, yard work or another form of physical exercise, but put the body to work regularly–at least three or four times weekly–for 30 minutes to 60 minutes each time. More is often better, but too much can be counterproductive so use some moderation. Somewhere between the extremes of zero exercise and competitive triathlon training can be a very wholesome and enjoyable amount of beneficial physical exercise for most people.

"But I hate to exercise. Taking more naps, I like that. Run more laps, no thanks." Well, doing one without doing the other denies you the dynamic, symbiotic impact of rigorous exercise and sufficient sleep/rest. The idea is to take more naps, not to take constant naps. The idea is to get more exercise, not to get constant exercise. The combined ideas would be to take more naps and to get more exercise, as an exercised body needs rest and a rested body is ready for exercise. "But I don't have any time. I'm too busy already. How can I fit in something else to my already packed schedule? When can I go to a gym with everything else I have to do?"

Those are realistic questions, but they are not convincing excuses or insurmountable barriers. Most people who exercise are busy people. How did they fit it into their schedule? They gave it a high priority and they put it on their schedule with the same certainty as going to work, eating meals, paying bills and sleeping. For those people exercise is a priority and a requirement rather than an option or a "when I can find the time" chance event.

"But I don't know anything about exercise. I never played a sport. I'm too old to learn something new." For people who are physically able to walk, no further knowledge, skill or training is needed. Walk through your neighborhood. Walk in the nearby shopping mall. Walk on a treadmill. Walk on an indoor track. Walk on an outdoor track. Walk up and down flights of stairs. Walk through the halls of a school or a mall. Walk through the halls of a church. Walk through a park. Walk in a lane of a swimming pool which gives the extra benefit of working against the water.

"But lifting weights is too hard. I can't pick up all that weight." Pick up two pounds in each hand and start. Then try five pounds in each hand. Then try eight pounds in each hand. Low weights combined with a high number of repetitions of an exercise can be very effective.

"But, well, you know…." Enough excuses. Read a book about exercise. Join a health club like the YMCA and get instruction. Agree with a friend or family member to exercise together and do not allow excuses. Start exercising, make exercise a habit and live better.

Run more miles was my plan for 28 years. I was a very devoted runner from March 1975 through May 2003. There were some milestones, personal bests, goals reached, goals missed and many experiences with "runners high." In 2003 my knees voted 2-1 against me. The knees said stop running. I said run, but I was outvoted.

A wonderful surprise awaited me as I temporarily gave up running and began rowing, swimming and using lots of new exercise machines. Only running has the "runner's high" glow after a glorious run, but there are more than enough alternatives to running for staying healthy. I did get bold in 2008 and returned to running, but with slower miles and in conjunction with a variety of exercise activities. The overall effect was more exercise, even when it could not all be running. There is merit in cross training.

So, run more miles, walk more miles, swim more laps, lift more weights, get up and move.

Today, I will get more exercise by doing this:

_____

18. OFFER MORE ENCOURAGEMENT

"You do a great job taking care of this place. I really appreciate it. I know it's hard work, but you are really good at it."

"Your technician just left my house. I wanted to call and let you know how polite and helpful he was. He called to let me know he was on the way. He cleaned up everything. He did great work. Please let his supervisor know."

"These are difficult spelling words. I'll practice them with you. We'll make flash cards. We'll even make a recording and you can listen to it. I know it will take some extra work, but you can do this. I'll be there with you."

"Listen, everybody gets nervous before their wedding. You two are a perfect couple, a match made in heaven. This is a busy week. We'll get it all done. You should enjoy every moment. You'll be a beautiful bride and a perfect wife. You know that he adores you. He'll be the husband you dreamed of when you were a little girl. We are all here for you."

"This is it. This is the state championship soccer game. We began preparing last July and being in this game tonight, winning this game tonight was our goal from the start. You are the best team in the state. Let's go prove that. I believe in you."

"It was a mistake. You were wrong to take your brother's bicycle without permission. He was very upset when he looked for it and it was gone. You had it, but he did not know that. You know what you should have done–leave the bike alone or get his permission. Now, you are a better person than this mistake so how can you correct this mistake and patch things up with your brother?"

"You are the right person for the job. If they select you, they select the best. If they pick someone else, it says that you don't want to work with people who are so mistaken and unfair. Give that interview all you've got. Your talent will be obvious. Go for it."

"You are in my thoughts and prayers. You did everything for your wife that was possible. For 57 years you were everything she needed. I can't imagine how much you miss her, but I can imagine how much she appreciated your love for 57 years. May your memories of your beloved wife give you joy and peace."

"You are right. That book is 112 pages long and it has lots of chapters. It will be the longest book you have ever read. Let's start together on the first chapter and then you read it on your own. You can do this."

"In the midst of the all the difficulties in our community, I'd like to thank you for the quality leadership you provide. You have a thankless job, so I thought someone should say thank you."

"You were always there for me after school when I needed help. I know I was difficult, but you taught me a lot. I heard someone say you might quit teaching. Please stay. There are many other students like me who need you."

Today I'll offer encouragement to

_____

by taking this action:

_____

19. CELEBRATE SMALL VICTORIES

"I lost one pound in eight days."

"My science grade went up from 71 to 80."

"I have not used vulgar language for two weeks."

"I reduced television watching to two hours each day. It used to be four or five hours."

"I saved $9 on groceries this week."

"I've been to church four weeks in a row."

"I've been early to work each day for one month. I was almost in trouble for being late so much."

"I reduced soft drinks to one can per day. I think I used to average three cans each day."

"I can say the alphabet all by myself."

"I did not make the varsity team, but I will probably be a starter on the junior varsity team. Going to those soccer camps this summer helped me make the team."

"Listen. Listen. I got a hole in one in miniature golf on a really, really hard hole. I've never done that before."

"We've saved enough in the past six months to buy the new sofa or to take the trip. We can't do both, but six months ago it was impossible to do either. Which do you prefer–the sofa or the trip?"

"I still have a little temperature and my head hurts some, but I'm not coughing and finally I can keep some food down."

"I got a bronze medal for bowling a game over 100. I always wanted to get a score over 100."

"Those tires look fine. You could get another 10,000 miles out of them. The battery is fine, too. All we had to do was change the oil and replace the headlight that was burned out. Actually you said to replace both headlight bulbs, so we did. The total is less than we had estimated. Not bad at all, I'd say."

"I'm so thankful that all of our family can be here together on Thanksgiving. It may seem like just one day out of the year, but just being together means the world to me. We don't need to go anywhere or do anything. Just being together is so good."

"I finished all of my homework. All of it!"

"The tests we ran raise some concerns, but there is nothing serious. Still, you have to eat healthy food, get exercise and quit smoking now. Those changes will help take care of you for now."

"Well, I did not get the promotion I wanted, but I got a 5 percent raise and a new project to manage. This could work out. I should be thankful to have a good job."

"Maybe we should visit that older couple around the corner and see if they need any help in their new home. I know you've wanted to meet them since they moved in. You were right. We should have visited them. Let's go now and make new friends."

"Johnny, you made up your bed all by yourself and without any reminder. I knew you could do it."

"I'm 13.5 years old today. Pretty special wouldn't you say?"

Today I will celebrate these small victories of mine or of someone else:

-
-
-
-
-
-
-
-
-

20. ELIMINATE MORE JUNK

Habits, thoughts, accumulated items. Boxes of materials that should have been thrown away years ago, but instead were pushed into a closet that will barely close due to more boxes of more materials being pushed into the same closet recently. Clutter in the basement, in the attic or in furniture's many drawers. Old routines that are counterproductive, but which linger due to inertia, not due to wisdom, productivity or beneficial results. Ideas that cause trouble or problems and which keep impacting actions that don't do any good for anyone.

"I always come in from work, watch a few TV shows, drink a few soft drinks and then, you know, order a pizza, roam around on the internet and go to sleep."

"It's a rat race every day. Get everyone up, dressed and fed. We both get ready for work, but we have to keep checking on the children and be sure they are ready for school. The phone rings. The dog is loose. The milk container is empty–how did I forget to buy milk? After school and after work it never slows down - soccer practice, piano lessons, walk the dog, homework to supervise, a meeting to attend, the orthodontist appointment may have to be rescheduled again. Something has to give and something has to go."

"Those people will never treat you fair. Don't be friends with them. I know they seem friendly to your face, but they'll turn on you. My brother knew them and he told me."

The easiest part of eliminating more junk may be to get rid of the unnecessary items that clog your closets, attic, basement, corners, cabinets, drawers or other hiding places. Donate, sell or throw away as much as possible. Keep what is truly meaningful for personal or family memories that each new generation should cherish. Eliminate the items that have no meaning, use or purpose.

Eliminating bad habits is not as easy, but it is possible. Select one bad habit, even if you have many, many bad habits, for now just select one. Then select one small improvement to make rather than telling yourself the habit will be 100 percent corrected today. For example, a person knows that they spend too much time watching television. For one week, television watching averaged two hours daily. This week, the person gets one hour of TV daily at the most. Plus, the new hour of time is applied in a better way such as work around the house, more time with the children, more time with spouse, reading a quality book or starting an exercise program.

How are junk ideas eliminated? A thought in place stays in place until acted on by a more powerful–true, beneficial, accurate, wise, wholesome–thought. For example–"I've been mad at you for weeks because I heard what you said about my brother. He's a good guy. Maybe you were just trying to impress your friends by trash talking my brother, but that was cheap. So, that's why I don't speak to you anymore. Do not call me or e-mail me again until you apologize and straighten this out. Yeah, I used to like you and I wanted to go out with you, but not now." If the recipient of that teenage e-mail does apologize, make amends and straighten everything out, lots of good could result. Adults may have comparable corrections to make with bad ideas.

Today I need to begin eliminating this junk:

_____

The action I can take today is

_____

And actions I'll take later are

_____

21. DREAM MORE DREAMS

Big, bold dreams. Little, minute-to-minute dreams. Dreams that last for a lifetime. Dreams that are updated monthly or annually. Glorious, lovely, wonderful, lively, wholesome, caring, daring, sharing, life-improving, joy spreading dreams.

There seems to be a common pattern in life that children and teenagers dream big dreams, college students and young adults dream fairly big dreams, middle aged adults dream only a few if any dreams and older adults encourage their grandchildren to dream big dreams. Maybe the passage of years and decades can "undream" a person, but that is not a requirement of getting older even if it is a common experience of getting older.

Thoreau was exactly right in his masterpiece, "Walden". "If we advance confidently in the direction of our dreams, we will meet with a success unexpected in common hours" and "If you have built castles in the air, that is where they belong, now put the foundations under them." Thoreau tells us to (A) advance confidently in the right direction–do not lose heart or lose courage, do not wander off the path or stray from the direct line to the target and (B) do the moment-to-moment, day-to-day, week-to-week work which establishes the foundation upon which a dream can securely stand.

A person dreams of getting a new job. There are endless actions to take which can become the foundation of the new job. Call, write, e-mail and visit everyone you know who could give you any insight, introduction or an interview. Ask people who work in your desired career how they got there and apply that advice. Persist–call, write, e-mail and visit again. Stand out from the crowd. Put your resume on the inside box top of a box containing 12 golf balls if you are applying to work in sports marketing and the person you would like to interview with helps manage a celebrity golf event to raise money for charity. Ask the person to use the golf balls as a prize at the charity fundraiser, to give you a volunteer job at the charity fundraiser, and to give you a job interview after the charity event.

A person dreams of losing 50 pounds. That may take one or two years of demanding work, but today reduce your typical calorie intake by 250 calories and increase your physical exercise so you burn up 250 more calories than usual. That is a minus 500 calories impact today. Repeat this for six more consecutive days for a total of one week worth of minus 500 calorie days. The result is a loss of one pound in one week. That is the day-to-day habit which can take you to the big dream.

A high school sophomore dreams of attending the best university in the country. Begin by getting a shirt, poster or other souvenirs from that school to serve as constant reminders of the dream. When friends ask you to join them for a Friday night wild and crazy party, you look at the shirt you are wearing and ask yourself–does this shirt say "wild and crazy party" or does it have the name of a college you hope to attend on it? You decide to go to the high school football game on Friday night with some friends and to go home right after that so you can get up early Saturday to continue some research in the library for a major assignment that is due in two weeks.

Interpretation of dreams we have while asleep is complicated and may be filled with as many guesses as insights. Still, it is revealing that the human being at rest does see mental pictures that intrigue, that arouse curiosity, that inspire, that confuse, that scare and that impress. We have built in dream capabilities, so we must be designed to dream.

My big or medium or small dream is

And today here's what I can do to take a step toward that dream:

---

22. GIVE MORE THANKS

For life itself
For another sunrise
For food to eat
For clothing
For shelter
For family
For cherished memories of loved ones who have died
For friends
For challenges
For great teachers who took an interest in you
For hope
For love
For faith
For the beauty of nature
For the peace of early morning
For the wonder of each new baby
For strength equal to our duties
For forgiveness given and received
For close call accidents that did not actually happen
For smiles
For pets
For the confidence to seek the seemingly or previously impossible
For birthdays
For three day weekends
For acts of kindness
For good music
For sacrifices made by parents, grandparents, and great-grandparents
For 50th wedding anniversaries
For humor
For courage
For people who do vital work in our community to protect people
and property
For second chances

For moments of solitude
For prayer
For big ideas
For enjoyable hobbies
For mountains and oceans and stars and all creation
For puppies
For wise advice
For an income
For someone to trust completely
For a soul mate
For promises made and kept
For medicine
For life, for each breath and for each heartbeat

I need to be more thankful for these blessings:

-

-

-

-

-

I can express my thanks by taking these actions:

-

-

-

-

-

23. REACH MORE CONCLUSIONS

"Well maybe, but I don't know. It might not work."

"That would take a lot of work. I've thought about it and I'll think about it some more. Check with me in a few weeks if the offer is still there."

"There's this other guy I sort of go out with, but it's not like he and I only date each other, but, you know, I mean, it's just strange and he might get mad."

"I'll do it tomorrow or next week. It can wait. There's no real hurry is there? Why do the work now when there is plenty of time?"

"I appreciate the job offer, but it's hard for me to decide right now. I guess I need more time and I guess you need a decision now."

"I'm going to pick up the phone right now and call her. We've dated for two years. We love each other. It's time to get married or break up. She's been vague sometimes and I've been vague sometimes, but we both need to reach a conclusion now. I know what I hope it will be. We belong together. We need to set the date and start plans for the marriage."

"It might be a good location for a new restaurant, but our other three locations are doing well and I really don't see this as the time to expand. Growth is usually good, but growing too fast can cause problems. We're successful so far. Let's always look for opportunities, but let's also not make a mistake because we acted too fast. The conclusion is not to buy that land now."

The human being is given the ability and the responsibility to think. Prior to any important action, decision or conclusion, much proper thinking is necessary. Then, there is a time to think and a time to conclude. After facts, opinion, research, insight, analysis of data, advice, counsel, prayer, discussion and one more night to sleep on it are completed, it is time to conclude. Such conclusions could include these:

- It is time to see the doctor
- It is time to change jobs

- It is time to refinance the mortgage
- It is time to get professional help
- It is time to move to a smaller house
- It is time to set up some new rules for our family
- It is time to buy a new car and replace the 12-year-old, 143,721 mile vehicle
- It is time to join a different church
- It is time to eat healthier food
- It is time to learn how to speak another language
- It is time to learn as much about computers as teenagers know
- It is time to move to another town
- It is time to quit thinking about moving to another town and make the very most of life right here

I need to reach conclusions about the following topics, issues, people, problems, opportunities, or about myself:

-

-

-

-

-

24. GET TO THE POINT

"Would you please get to the point," Angela said.

"Sure, the point is that I don't like those two trees in the front yard. I've never liked them. They are too big. They looked OK when we moved here 14 years ago, but they grow and grow each year. They grow more than the tree companies can cut off no matter how often we pay to have that done. I say we just remove the trees." David had gotten to the point.

"Great idea, David. The trees are too big. Next spring or fall we might do some simple landscape work to fill in, but we do waste money each year on those trees. It's time for them to go."

Get to the point.

"Show me the math homework you've been working on. We agreed that I would check it at 8:00 tonight. It is 8:00, so let's see how you did." Dad was clear in his words and calm in his tone.

"About that math. You see, I, well, I………."

"Kim, get to the point. Where's the homework. We agreed on 8:00 as the time. I'm here now right on time."

"Dad, I'm not finished, it's like, I mean……………"

"Kim, get to the point."

"Ok, Dad. I haven't started yet. I know. It's my fault. I was on the phone and on the internet. Here, take the phone. I've already turned off the computer. In 30 minutes I'll have it done. I'm sorry."

"Kim, I'll keep the cell phone until that math homework is completed, turned in, graded and returned to you and to me. Be sure the grade is A or B. And it's time the computer went back to the family room. You can use it there and your mother or I will know."

"I understand, Dad. Math is easy."

"Kim, since math is easy you could have finished it before now. See you in 30 minutes. I'll take the computer now. You'll know where to find it."

Get to the point. "I'm sorry. I was wrong. How can I make it up to you?" That statement, spoken honestly and sincerely, puts the emphasis and the action on solving a problem or resolving a conflict.

"Well, it's not my fault. You could have called me. Why do I always have to call you? I know, I usually do call, but I just forgot this time and I was late and I had other things on my mind. But it's not all my fault." That statement just prolongs, expands and complicates the issue.

It is worth noting that getting to the point can be done politely and diplomatically. Getting to the point is not an excuse for being harsh or rude. "Here's the deal. For every hour you practice the piano you get one-fourth of an hour of video game time. You have talent and skills with both, so work on both. We aren't negotiating this." Fair, firm, to the point and avoids any explosive "Turn off that awful video game and start playing the piano now. What's wrong with you? Can't you do anything you are told?"

Getting to the point can challenge our intention to be diplomatic and polite. When we see ourselves or someone we care about making a major mistake, it is difficult, but sometimes essential, to insist that actions stop and the mistake be avoided, especially if prior efforts were ignored. "Listen, you eat too much. We have discussed this so many times. That's all there is to it. You eat too much. You know it, your family knows it, your friends know it. The doctor has talked to you. This has to stop. Do you prefer going to a professional counselor or to a group meeting? Your choice. I'll go with you. But one of those happens this week. I care about you enough to insist on this." Direct, yet caring. Firm, but supportive. Blunt, but softer and gentler statements earlier were ignored. No vulgarity or anger, just certainty emphasized.

"I'm proud of you." "Great job." "I love you." "Way to go." "Thank you so much." "You made my day." Those comments also get to the point and make points that might be passed over in the busy pace of a typical day, but that need and merit frequent use.

Today I need to get to the point about

_____

and I will do that this way:

_____

25. OPEN MORE DOORS

A literal application of the idea "Open more doors" could mean to be sufficiently aware, sensitive, thoughtful and polite that we hold a door open for the person who is walking right behind us. Going further, we make the effort to hold a door open for someone who, though not right behind us, is within our sight and clearly could use help getting through a closed door. Maybe that person is guiding several young children or is carrying a heavy load, is on crutches or just walks very slowly due to old age. This application of open more doors can include those times when many people are going through a door in succession and each person pushes the door back enough so the door does not slam in the face of the next person.

In all of these cases, it is quite proper, honorable, friendly, caring, kind and polite to open more doors for people who will benefit from that momentary act of kindness. Smiles and goodwill are created at the cost of a very little time, zero money, but a sensitive outlook toward other people.

A creative application of the idea of open more doors could relate to circumstances such as these.

- A capable person is seeking a job, but so far all doors are closed to an interview for the desired job.
- An accomplished high school student finds that some colleges and universities eagerly open their doors for serious consideration of the student's application while other schools appear to close their admission doors to this student.
- That a community activist who is being encouraged to seek a local political office finds some support, but that other doors actually are closed shut or forcefully slammed in response to any approach by this hopeful candidate.
- That a young adult gentleman who is certain that he has met the woman of his hopes, prayers and dreams finds no open doors as she politely refuses to make any acknowledgement of his interest. Although they have been cordial acquaintances, she just shows no interest in a

date with him. The gentleman in question is completely unaware that another delightful lady at the company where they all three work would be very pleased to go out with him.

In situations such as these, how can closed doors become open? Imagine a 53-year-old person whose company offers an early retirement package that is too good to pass up. After 28 years with this company, the offer is accepted. The person decides, "You know, I went straight into the army after high school. I served for seven years. Then I worked for 28 years at the company. You know what, I'm going to college at the big university right here in town. They have about 30,000 students and they can make room for one more. I never did and now I will. Plus, I'm going to be the first 53-year-old college freshman to play college soccer. It's been 10 years since I played soccer on the company team in that recreational league, but let's make a comeback."

Will the door to a college education be open to this person? Very likely. Colleges increasingly educate "non-traditional" students whose circumstances in life make higher education appealing, attractive, affordable or necessary at stages of life other than a few months after high school graduation.

Will the door to playing college soccer at a major university which aggressively recruits the nation's best soccer players and which gives college scholarships to those soccer players be open to this 53-year-old would-be sports superstar who seeks a return to soccer after a 10 year absence? Probably not but perhaps it is worth a try, yet caution is advised. The university may have a wide-open door for intramural sports and may have lots of physical exercise equipment available to everyone. Those options are more likely to work and to have open doors.

Open more doors includes some element of thinking big, but also an element of being practical in our pursuits. Opening more doors successfully works better when doors are put in the easy, difficult and impossible categories. There are inspiring stories of determined people who made the impossible happen, but most pursuits of the impossible probably end in little achievement.

Pursuit of the difficult can result in much more achievement. Our Romeo friend may never get to go out with the Juliet of his dreams, but the Janet who dreams of going out with Romeo could truly be the dream Romeo should hope for and be thrilled about.

Today I need to work on opening this door:

_____

The action I will take today is

_____

26. END MORE FAILURES

Remove the causes of failure and you increase the possibility of success. What are the causes of failure? Some are listed below, but the reader should add more causes at the end of this list.

- Making a quick decision before doing enough proper thinking
- Acting purely out of emotion
- Making decisions without getting enough good advice and wise counsel
- Procrastination
- Making excuses
- Cheating
- Violating the law
- Being immoral, illegal or just plain stupid
- Thinking that even though something sounds too good to be true it really could be true
- Going deep into debt
- Being dishonest
- Insufficient practice or preparation
- Being lazy
- Use of drugs
- Thinking that "It can't happen to me"
- Ignoring the wisdom given by grandparents, parents and guardians
- Taking excessive, unwise risks
- Mismanagement of money
- Wasting time
- Not planning
- Acting before thinking
- Speaking before thinking

What does a person do to end more failures? One place to start is by identifying a particular failure that has happened recently and that perhaps has happened repeatedly. A student recently failed a high school geometry test. The same student failed a high school chemistry test a month ago. The student quit the cross country team recently after doing poorly in a very important competition. There are many questions to ask–is he studying for tests, is he getting enough sleep, is there any indication of drug use, did he break up with his girlfriend, is there a problem at home, did he lose his part-time job? There are reasons for the recent problems. Those reasons can be identified and resolved. Removing the causes of those problems and the failure associated with them can increase the possibility of success.

"We're thinking about getting married. We love each other and stuff, but we're not sure yet about marriage. It concerns us both that we are each from divorced parents. We have wonderful parents, but their divorces kind of concern us. We have not seen a good marriage in our homes. We don't want our marriage to fail." That couple is wise to seek expert counsel before considering being engaged and then married. A marriage counselor, a pastor, a couple celebrating their 50th wedding anniversary, and their own parents perhaps giving the wisdom that comes from difficulty, are sources to consider.

An athletic team which fails in an important game will study the statistics, the film, the individual effort, the team effort, and will find corrections to make. That process can work in other parts of life, also.

Here's a list of failures I need to end:

_____

Here's what caused those failures:

_____

Here's what needs to be done to end those failures:

_____

_____

By the way, study and analyze successes also. What caused the success? Did the overall success hide any part of the endeavor which could have been done better?

27. IMPLEMENT MORE IMPROVEMENTS

When people are asked what improvements they would like to make in their lives, the realistic emphasis is on the word "make" not on the word "improvements." Progress, achievements, results and improvements are parts of life that are caused, are made and are made to happen. Progress, achievements, results and improvements do not just appear. Still, it is common to consider the what before considering the how. So let's list some improvements that could be commonly mentioned by people of various ages and please add to the list at the end.

- Lose weight
- Make more money
- Make better grades at school
- Get promoted at work
- Get a better job somewhere else
- Get married
- Buy a house
- Get a new car
- Get in better physical shape
- Read more good books
- Volunteer more time to worthwhile causes
- Spend more time with my children
- Communicate better with my spouse
- Go to church
- Watch less television
- Learn to play bridge, tennis, soccer, chess
- Start a new hobby
- End a bad habit
- Control my temper
- Use no vulgar language
- Smile more
- Stay out of trouble
- Do all my homework on time, correctly and completely
- Be more polite

A good idea or a good goal not implemented is of little or no worth. The challenge is to select a very beneficial improvement and to implement it effectively beginning now. As an example, use the improvement of spending more time with your children. What is keeping you from doing that?

1. The children are at school and you are at work. Go have lunch with your children at school. Go visit a class at school.

2. The children are outside playing and you are inside watching television. Turn off the television and go play with the children outside.

3. You are going to play a five hour round of golf. Change that to taking the children with you to a driving range and teach them to play golf.

4. Your idea:

_____

To every problem there is an equal and opposite solution. The greatest challenges in making improvements often include not identifying the problem that needs to be solved or not identifying the improvements to be made. Yet, the greatest challenge is to implement–take action, put into action, do the improvement. So to help with implementation it can be beneficial to take small steps. To lose weight, for example, substitute water for sugar soft drinks. Then eliminate desserts. Then start exercising. Implement a big improvement by implementing small parts of the big improvement one at a time.

The improvement I need to make is

_____

And that means I must implement this today:

_____

28. WATCH MORE SUNRISES

I once said to a friend who is an amazingly talented, creative, gifted, inspiring and profound writer, "you do with words what the sunrise does with the morning." Let's consider just what the sunrise does with and for the morning. Please add your thoughts at the end of the list:

- Gives life to it
- Defines it
- Makes each one unique
- Attracts favorable attention to it
- Inspires awe of it
- Creates appreciation of it
- Illuminates it
- Releases it from darkness
- Liberates it
- Shapes, guides and impacts it while still leaving unlimited possibilities
- Escorts it
- Announces it
- Introduces it
- Reveals it
- Encourages it
- Expresses part of it
- Interacts with it
- Makes it possible
- Works with it, helps it start and then releases it
- Is part of it

So why should we watch more sunrises? One reason is that the sunrise could do with us and for us what the sunrise already does with and for the morning. Consider this perspective and challenge offered as if the sunrise could speak to us.

"Good morning. Let's get to the point–I've done my job today. Now, you get up, get going and do your job. I've illuminated the start of the day. Now, you move through that light directly in pursuit of the duties you have. I'm going to be with you for part of the day and I'll return tomorrow, but while I'm here we share the work and when I'm gone it is all up to you."

How is a sunrise most effectively, enjoyably and beneficially watched? Of course, wear sunglasses and never look directly at the sun. Some people may live by a beach and can watch the beauty of the horizon changing into the first glimpse of daylight. Others may live by mountains and can see the total darkness of night become the vibrant light shining on the mountains. Others may live in a typical town where walking through the neighborhood enables you to savor the sensations and the signals of sunrise. Others, due to physical limitations, may need to rely on indirect indications of morning's arrival. Still, a new day dawns as welcomed and previewed by the wonderful reliability of, the beauty of, the inspiration of and the challenge of a new sunrise.

Today I will carefully watch the sunrise by taking this action:

_____

Today I will respond to the challenge, hope and inspiration of the sunrise's call to action by

_____

29. AVOID STUPIDITY

"I ate too much, I am stuffed. I feel sick."

"I wasted so much money. I had plenty of clothes already. Why did I buy more clothes?"

"I can't believe I said that. I'll be in trouble forever now." Mistakes–stupid actions–are rarely forced upon us. We make mistakes. The human will never fully eliminate mistakes, but some can be prevented, others can be reduced, minimized or avoided.

Stupidity can be avoided or, at least, minimized.

Our only real opponent is yesterday. Ask yourself: Am I doing everything in my life better today than I did everything in life yesterday? If the answer is yes always, or almost always, you win. Everyone can win in an individualized challenge to surpass yesterday.

I made some mistake yesterday. Whatever that mistake was, it is my opponent today. I will take the necessary action to not repeat that mistake. I will take the necessary action to correct that mistake. I will take the necessary action to limit the impact of yesterday's mistake to yesterday, so if at all possible yesterday's mistake does not impact today, except as a lesson learned and now applied.

Some mistakes happen despite the best thinking, the wisest advice and the smartest decisions. Unexpected events occur and what made perfect sense at one time may make no sense now. You work for a very successful company for 17 years and are having a productive career. The top executives commit such severe fraud that the company goes bankrupt. Was it a mistake to work there for 17 years? No, based on everything you knew, saw and did it was sensible to work there. Was it a mistake for the top executives to commit fraud? Yes. They were wrong and whatever they deceived themselves into thinking they were going to achieve through illegal and immoral actions was bad, wrong, against the law, unethical and just plain stupid.

When stupidity happens the best action is to correct it. Do not cover up stupidity with more stupidity. Example–many historians and political observers are convinced that if very early in the Watergate criminal ordeal, President Nixon had said to the nation, "I was wrong. I was stupid, I made mistakes. Here is the plan to completely resolve and correct this series of stupid mistakes" he could have stayed in office. Instead he and others made repeated mistakes and the accumulated volumes of those completely unethical, illegal, unnecessary and totally stupid mistakes destroyed a president and have caused decades of lingering difficulties.

What is the opposite of stupid? Smart. Wise. Brilliant. Those words are close. The opposite of stupid is thorough, redundant, meticulous, honest, ethical, moral thinking which leads to a proper decision, action or conclusion. Does that type of thought require time and work? Yes, but it is far less time and work than would come from attempting to correct the results of a mistake, of being stupid.

Avoid stupidity.

Parts of my life I need to avoid stupidity with:

_____

How I will avoid stupidity in those parts of my life:

_____

How I can, generally, avoid stupidity:

_____

30. BE LESS SELFISH

"I'm very sorry to hear that someone vandalized your car. I guess it could happen to any of us who work here and park nearby, but it's just wrong for it to happen. I asked everyone to donate something to help you pay the insurance deductible. Here's $217 from people who care about you and who really appreciate you."

"No, it's OK. I can easily change my schedule. I'll pick you up and take you to your doctor's appointment. It will be good to visit with you."

"Wow. That's a really neat pair of shoes. I really like those. You look like a basketball star."

"Sometimes life hurts, it just hurts. There's not much I can do, except be here and cry with you. I'll stay as long as you need me."

"Congratulations. I'm so glad the job interview went well for you. I hope you get the job."

"I'll clean up the kitchen. You had a rougher day than any of us. The children are in their rooms reading. You relax."

"I know we promised delivery of the new washing machine by this morning. Two people are sick and one truck broke. Listen, I'm bringing it myself right now, plus I'm bringing you a $25 gift certificate to our store."

"I'll help."

"I can volunteer to do that."

"We have some clothes we can donate."

"Sure, I'll be there."

"No, I can't go on that fishing trip. I promised the boys and my wife that this weekend was all family."

"I don't need a new television as much as the church building fund needs a contribution."

"It's the last brownie. You take it, please."

"How could I help?"

"It's our anniversary, sweetheart, tell me anything you'd like to do and it's done."

The wisdom of the ages is forever true. "Do unto others as you would have them to unto you."

Here are actions I can take to be less selfish:

Today:

Tomorrow:

Next Week:

Always:

31. WHISTLE MORE SONGS

Does anybody whistle these days? As you sit on a train, bus, subway, or airplane, do you hear anyone whistling a song? While walking down the street, do you whistle a familiar tune or even a random assortment of musical notes? Where did whistling go?

A person who does whistle a tune is apt to get peculiar looks which could translate into observations such as "What's she so happy about?" or "Who does he think he is? Some famous musician?" or "I wish he'd stop that noise."

I'm absolutely certain that as a child I noticed person after person who would whistle pleasant tunes as they walked along the street, as they shopped in a store, as they sold products door to door, as they walked, as they drove a car, as they just passed the time.

Maybe the invention of radios with individual earplugs began the decline of people who whistle. Maybe the popularity of portable cassette tape players and then of portable CD players - with headsets of course–did to whistling a song what e-mail did to writing and mailing a letter. Maybe new electronic devices with endless downloads were the final attack on whistled music.

Amid the noise of current life from sounds of traffic to cell phones ringing, from telemarketer calls to remote entry devices for cars, from pagers to aircraft, from alarm clocks to cable television talk shows, from urban sprawl to barking dogs in the neighborhood, from machinery to shouts, it could be quite charming and cheerful to whistle a few notes, a melody, a song or a tune.

A crowded elevator might not be the place to start. Walking through a shopping mall, walking through the halls at school, walking along sidewalks on the way to lunch, moments such as these could be enhanced when a tune is whistled.

No matter what tune is selected or what quality the whistled version of the tune reaches, it is common that hearing whistling can inspire a moment of joy, of peace, of pleasure. Plus, if you whistle you are a participant in the music of the moment.

If you hear an inspiring song at church on Sunday, whistle it throughout the week.

If your child performs in a musical presentation at school, whistle one of their songs all week.

If you and your spouse have a favorite song, whistle it occasionally - maybe often - as a reminder of its meaning to both of you.

There are other good times and good places where a moment of a day could be enhanced if you whistle. Think of some times, places and moments like those, pause and list them below, but first take a few moments right now and whistle. Neat, huh!? Liked it, didn't you? Continue, please.

Note: There are times and places to not whistle, to not speak, to be very silent, please.

32. GAZE AT STARS

Stars in the sky are always there, always present, always in existence; however, stars are revealed at night. Always there, but seen only under certain circumstances. There is some powerful insight in this reality. How can we apply it?

First, gaze at stars for more than a few minutes. The longer you watch, the more you see. Perhaps that is also true about characteristics that we can appreciate in people. The more we look into the eyes, the heart, the mind, the soul, the personality, the life of a person, the more we realize, see and can appreciate about that person. Another application could be with a hobby such as golf, bridge, sewing or gardening. At first glance such activities may seem unappealing, but those hobbies attract millions of devoted participants. Looking into the hobby with the depth and the appreciation of a practitioner can reveal much goodness about the activity that a quick, superficial glance cannot show.

Second, gaze at the stars and think of the questions that people through the centuries have asked, probed, explored, pondered and wondered about regarding stars. What is a star? What did ancient cultures think stars were? Did people worship stars? Did people think that stars were temporary? Why did people assign names to stars and names to constellations of stars? Were stars seen as powerful, as potentially impacting earth from starry places of new life?

Third, just let the mind travel through time, space, thought, imagination and beyond all limits. The stars give a preview of infinity, of eternity, of always, of no restrictions. What does the mind do when we inspire it to think with such illuminated liberation?

Gazing at the stars is often done while standing. Some people sit in a chair. Everything about star gazing changes when you lie down on the ground and look up. You see from east to west, from north to south, from now to forever.

Gaze at the stars knowing that a night sky without stars would be blank, stark, discouraging, empty and alone. Know also that a night sky filled with stars is ample evidence that the universe is artistically made, is seeking our attention, offers to stir our imagination, fascinate our mind, relax our body, warm our heart and majestically enliven our soul.

With no admission fee, we can gaze at the stars and secure priceless insight about life, people, truth, hope, wonder, thinking and ourselves. Gaze at the stars and you gaze at the sacred, beautiful, lovely inspiring possibility of perfection or, perhaps, an example of perfection itself.

33. MAKE CHANGES NOW

To make the future different from the past it is necessary to make changes in the present right here, right now. A revolution immediately is not required. Small steps of change can add up to large adventures of progress.

Taking smaller steps of gradual, incremental, possible change is not watering down the ultimate goal and is not lowering the standard of performance. What is lowered is the height of each step. The distance from where we are today to where we will eventually arrive does not change. The size of and the number of steps which will get us to our desired goal does change.

Example: A person decides to lose 50 pounds. The plan is to lose two pounds per week in each of the next 25 weeks. It works for two weeks and then they can't tolerate the severe diet and the severe exercise plan. They then gain four pounds in one week and have really accomplished nothing except frustration.

Far better would be to lose 50 pounds in 50 weeks. 50 small, possible, realistic steps that can be taken make more sense than attempting 25 too steep, too difficult, too unrealistic steps that result in failure.

Making changes now means making possible changes. Right here, right now you can call a friend you have been out of touch with for months. Call the person now. Agree to visit soon. The friendship needs to be nourished, restored and nurtured. Calling daily could easily be too much. Calling annually is too little. Call now, then call occasionally, often or regularly. Make the change now from being out of touch to being in touch.

"I'm going to drop out of school right now. I quit." That may sound like an example of making a change now, but it is actually making a mistake now. The change to make is to ask a school teacher, counselor or principal for advice, ideas, options and guidance on how to stay in school, how to endure school, how to succeed in school and how to benefit from school. The next change is to do what those people advise, which is a change from what you have been doing.

"I will call my wife once each day during work hours. I called her all the time when we were dating. I never call her now like I used to. I can still do boyfriend acts of kindness. I will change now and call her."

List below, please, some proper, good, wholesome, beneficial, possible changes you can make now. List also why the change is needed and what exactly will be done now.

-
-
-
-
-
-
-
-

34. SAY MORE PRAYERS

Throughout human history people have prayed, worshipped, meditated, studied sacred writing, pondered myths, heard legends, appealed to the gods, listened to prophets, sought God, pursued holy truth. In many traditions, ceremonies, rituals, practices, commitments, services or quests people have acknowledged that there is more to the human adventure than the physical and the mental. The soul, the spirit, the spiritual are vital parts of the human longing for meaning, peace, purpose, direction and help.

Given that premise, there is benefit in the advice to say more prayers. Questions immediately arise: (1) to whom is the prayer directed, offered, sent, (2) how is the prayer to be prayed, (3) how is the prayer to be answered or will it be answered and (4) what if I never pray?

This short essay is not designed as a theological treatise; rather as a practical acceptance that the history of mankind includes a convincing body of evidence that through the ages of centuries past and into the very present moment, a common part of the human experience has been to seek contact with, assurance from, help from, wisdom from and truth from a larger-than-human-life aspect of life itself. From mythology to legend, from scripture to prophet, from soothsayer to oracle, the prayerful endeavor continues. To whom people pray will vary. The motivations to pray have more similarities.

Different traditions will expect various methods of prayer— eyes closed, head bowed, knees bent, arms raised, total silence, gentle music, in a tranquil room, outdoors, on a set schedule, at any moment of any day. There are as many variations in forms of prayer as there are in teachings about prayer.

Is prayer answered? If yes, how is prayer answered? If no, why pray? One perspective says that prayer itself is its own answer. To pray is to answer because the fact that we pray answers questions about our understanding of life and gives indications of our priorities, hopes, fears, needs, values and incompleteness. To pray confirms that we are going outside of ourselves, our thoughts, our resources in search of that which surpasses our human abilities.

How will a response come from what or whom our prayers are sent? To limit that answer to written or spoken words is to limit in human terms the options, the methods, the source, the power of the recipient of our prayer. When we look at the sunset we do not have to hear it say "I'm beautiful, I'm amazing, I'm signaling the end of the day and the beginning of the night." We already understand that about the sunset. Perhaps the return message of prayer is similar.

What happens if a person never prays? That person misses a wholesome part of the human experience which for centuries has brought hope, peace, meaning and joy to many, many people. Why miss that? Say more prayers.

Early today I will pray about these topics:

-
-
-
-

Then later today I will say more prayers which will be about these topics:

-
-
-
-

35. SHARE MORE MEALS

It might be easy, but still inaccurate, to think of the "take more naps" approach to life as lazy. One nap after another nap would miscommunicate that a life of naps is the intent. A healthy life of proper action, proper rest and proper development of heart, mind, body and soul are the characteristics of a "take more naps" perspective.

Consider a child who emphatically says, "But Mommy we saw the pictures. Those little children are so hungry you could see their bones. They never smiled. Can't we help them, please? We have enough. Can't we send them some food, please? We have to, Mommy, we have to share."

The response to that genuine appeal to help feed the hungry is not to say, "Honey, you're upset about those pictures. Just go play and you'll feel better." The response is in this category, "Honey, I really appreciate your concern for those hungry children. There are ways we could help. Some charities and churches in our town collect money to help groups that feed hungry people. Remember when you had a lemonade stand last summer to make money to buy your new baseball glove and baseball bat? Well, you could have another lemonade sale to raise money for a charity or church."

"Yeah, Mom, let's do that. Let's do that right now."

In terms of arithmetic or mathematics, if the total amount of food on planet Earth prepared, served and eaten in one day was equally divided among all people who live on planet Earth, there would probably be enough for everyone to have ample food for the day. That allocation approach will never occur and should never occur because it negates the motivation of capitalism, which the American adventure confirms is the most productive of all economic systems and is the most energetic of all economic engines. The abundance created by capitalism, if compassionately shared with people in need, can confirm the benefits of capitalism and can defeat hunger. The twin foundations of capitalism and its political counterpart democracy are freedom and responsibility. People who are free from hunger have the responsibility to assist those who are burdened by hunger. This is a moral, ethical and humane necessity. This is also practical. Hungry people think only of hunger. Hungry people may turn to crime. Hungry people are unable to contribute work, taxes, volunteer time or other beneficial actions because hunger dominates their life. To become free from hunger could then enable a person to become ready, willing and able to participate productively in the community–local, national or international.

Share more meals has one other important meaning. Families benefit from sharing meals with each other. A fast food society where meals are shared at the drive-through window and in the car while frantically dashing through traffic from meeting to meeting, activity to activity, event to event denies itself the joy of tranquil time together at the supper table. Just as soccer practices and piano lessons and church committee meetings–plus other endless demands–are scheduled by busy families, the take more naps concept says take more time to share more meals as a family.

Put the meal times on the family's master schedule and work other events around the meal times. Deep, lasting, daily, real interaction is not accomplished via voice mail, notes on the refrigerator or e-mails and text messages between family members or between friends. Sit down. Share a meal. Look at each other, listen to each other. Talk with each other. Do this often, regularly, sincerely and with joy. Share more meals together with family and you build the family. In truth that sharing is not primarily about the meal, it's about the people.

Today I can provide more meals to hungry people by taking these actions:

_____

Today, this week, this month, I can share more meals with my family by taking these actions:

_____

36. PLAY MORE GAMES

Years ago, the perfect solution to a rainy Saturday afternoon was for parent and child, brother and sister, grandparent and grandchild to find the checkers game and play. That might lead to playing card games next and then to learning about chess. When a snack was needed, maybe some cookies would be baked or some popcorn popped. If everyone in the family joined in, the game choices might expand to include board games that four people can participate in. The results would include enjoyment of the game, winning some games and losing others, anticipating the taste of freshly baked cookies and experiencing the family goodness of being together.

Checkers and chess are still around. Those games might be in boxes stored in a crowded closet or in a dusty attic. Cookies can still be baked at home with all of the smiles which helping in the kitchen provided for previous generations. Board games are still enjoyable and can be educational. So, despite the busy schedules of today, the electronic versions of games and the old-fashioned image of baking cookies at home, there is much joy to be found in the pure simplicity of checkers, warm chocolate chip cookies and time together.

Play more games. "Let's go see a movie." "Let's go to the mall." "Let's go to the amusement park. The new roller coaster is so neat." "Let's go to that new electronic tag place." "Let's go to the big arcade and pizza place." "Let's sit on the floor, set up everyone's favorite board game and play each game once. We'll pop popcorn, make lemonade and bake some cookies. It's perfect for a rainy day like today. Plus, it will cost about $3 instead of the $40 or $50 or $100 or more that the other ideas would cost."

Of course, it is enjoyable to go see a movie or to go to another pay-per-laugh place, but staying at home, being with family and friends, actually interacting with each other as part of the game, deserves more consideration than it may usually get. Years ago when a grandfather and a grandchild played checkers, it was about much more than which piece to move and who won. It was about being together, about learning from each other and learning about each other. It was about a tranquil pace that enhanced conversation, it was about sharing time and sharing ourselves.

Sometimes it may have seemed that the checkers game was the center of attention, but that was an illusion. The people were the real center of attention. Movies and amusement parks can sometimes become more noticed than the people who go there.

Play more games. Play more games together. Play more games and create more wholesome interaction and capture the joy of sharing time together playfully.

It's an unusually sunny and warm Sunday afternoon in late October. A dear friend had anticipated the good weather and suggested a tennis game for 1:00 in the afternoon. I made myself say yes because it is too easy to miss such a beautiful afternoon and to miss a lovely friendship. The work I needed to do would get completed later in the afternoon. I decided to play more games and the blessing surpassed any other use of that time. Lesson learned–play more games.

37. READ MORE GOOD BOOKS

Twenty-four years ago I read the words that changed how I think, how I work, how I hope, how I solve problems, how I plan, how I believe and how I live. The words were written in 1917 by my great-grandmother to go with a Bible she gave her son. She wrote them for her son, my grandfather. I have the family keepsake Bible which those words were placed in.

"Remember, love who gave you this,
When other days shall come.
When she who had thy earliest kiss
Sleeps in her narrow home,
Remember, 'twas a mother gave
The gift to one she would die to save.
That mother sought a pledge of love,
The holiest, for her son,
And from the gifts of God above
She chose a goodly one.
She chose for her beloved boy
The source of life and light and joy."

The words captured my total attention. "The source of life." Source is a powerful idea. Source of life is a powerful idea. My great-grandmother physically gave life itself to my grandfather and with a gift on his 21st birthday gave him wisdom about the source of all life. If you understand the source of anything, you understand the item itself. How obvious. I had sought for years to manage life correctly without fully understanding that the source of life will manage its creation if creation obeys and cooperates and defers.

A book. A few words in a book. A book of ancient truth, forever true. An expression of love forever real. I'll give this same book to the next generation in our family. That could occur 100 years after my great-grandmother gave the book and her personal inscription to my grandfather. Five generations of life living the same love, the same truth, the same faith, the same hope.

All of this is made possible because decades ago in 1917 a mother expressed love to her son. In so doing a great-grandmother expressed wisdom to her great-grandson. What is that wisdom? To make life work as it should, go to the source of life. Doing that helps make every part of life different and better.

Read more good books, including those with a wise inscription from years ago, but which speak forever.

There are, of course, many good books to read - fiction and fact, literature and history, adventure and biography, how-to advice books and political commentary books. There are books you read years ago which merit a second reading. There are current bestsellers which deserve immediate attention. There are books on a shelf at your home which cry out for your attention. Until every good book has been read, why watch more and more television? TV shows rarely impact lives for good. Read more books. Take notes, write ideas in the margins. Stop and re-read a strong paragraph. Think, dream, learn, realize, imagine, remember, question, reflect, decide, take action.

Read more good books and do what they say. The wisdom of the ages is in print. Put that wisdom in your mind and in your life. Read more good books. Good includes wholesome, beneficial, informative, inspiring and educational. Reading good books can help us be good people. There are good books to embrace and bad books to avoid. Read more good books.

38. SEND MORE LETTERS

It is possible that in quality, and perhaps in quantity also, more is accomplished by people who are consistently good than by people who are occasionally great. The few occasions of greatness which fluctuate with more occasions of ordinary, or below average or poor performance combine to give an unpredictable, unreliable, erratic result.

The same idea applies with interpersonal communication. Imagine that you hear from a wonderful friend or relative once per year. On this occasion, the friend visits you in person, takes you to the finest restaurant, asks endless questions about you and your life, takes you to a clothing store to give you your choice of the finest clothes, concludes the day by taking you to a spectacular theater performance and takes you home ending this glorious day by saying, "Take care. Have a great year. See you in 365 days."

Consider another wonderful friend or relative who never treats you to any of those thrilling activities, but who is consistently kind to you, thoughtful toward you, available to you, in touch with you and very consistently shares time, concern, events and communication with you. Imagine that this person, every week or two, writes you a letter, an old-fashioned pen and paper letter, which is sent to you through the post office, that's right, through the mail.

You get home, find that letter, sit down to read it, smile, read it again, smile again and experience a gentle, genuine connection with that person. You decide to write them back and you notice how carefully you select your words, how naturally your thoughts and feelings flow, how an unexpected idea comes to your mind through the inspirational thought process which writing to one person enhances.

You remember your grandmother telling you once that it was the frequent letters your grandfather sent to her through the mail that won her 21-year-old heart many decades ago. You wonder if e-mail can do the same and then you answer your own question–communication at the speed of electronics serves many important purposes, but, communication at the speed of paper and pen thinking can include a depth, a reflection, a time produced thoughtfulness which the pace, speed and nature of electronic communication may not support as easily.

Write more letters. In the attic of many homes are treasured letters written so long ago across the miles, across the oceans, across the years, across the feelings and across the hearts, minds and souls of the dear people who corresponded. With pen in hand and ideas moving from the mind to the fingers, we simply experience a different type, quality and purpose of communication. This is communication which we can hold on to physically, emotionally and through the years.

Write more letters including thank you notes, thinking of you notes, get well soon notes, I love you notes, I miss you notes, I need your advice letters, I'm thinking of you letters, I'm so sorry letters and many more.

Write more letters. Go to a desk or table, use paper and a pen or pencil. Hand write an old fashioned letter which will be mailed via the post office. The communication that comes through the written word is unique. Be unique. Send more letters.

39. WATCH MORE SUNSETS

The radiant and glorious colors of the sunset presented a heavenly masterpiece that no human artist could fully reproduce, but which every observant human could find inspiration from. There was more to come as the artistry of nature continued. The fading, slumbering, final touches of sunset colors pointed to the emerging sliver of the moon which was joined by the planet Venus at its brightest vibrance. It appeared as if you could stand with one foot on the moon, the other foot on Venus and reach out to embrace the universe.

Observing this wonder of nature touched my heart, soul, mind and body. Observing this wonder of nature required no admission cost other than my time, my attention and my thoughts. I then realized what priceless gifts those are to give to people–our time, our total attention, our continuous thoughts.

Watch more sunsets, but watch them whenever possible with another person, with your spouse, with your children, with friends, with an older person whose time is often spent within the boundaries of isolation and four compressed walls, with a child who will ask endless and creative questions about the sunset and watch them with a person you love but with whom the initial words of love have not yet been spoken.

Watch more sunsets and be patient as you watch. Permit no schedule or cell phone to take you from this purposeful gazing into the infinity of nature's artistry which is God's creation. A sunset is not to be glanced at or quickly acknowledged. Sunsets are to be savored, consumed, experienced and memorized.

In watching a sunset, the careful viewer sees more than the ending of daylight and the beginning of nightfall. The intent and intense observer sees the majestic wonder and beauty, the unique colors and shapes, the inspiring and hopeful call to tranquility.

Watch more sunsets and in doing this pay attention closely to the thoughts, hopes, ideas, dreams, prayers and wisdom which come to you. Be aware also of the universe which includes the sunset and includes you plus so much more.

It is a miraculous universe. Watch more sunsets and give more thanks for each sunset–past, present and future–shared with mankind by the creator of all sunsets.

40. NOTICE MORE MIRACLES

I walked into a large bookstore on a Tuesday evening with no real intention of buying anything. Christmas was two days away, but my shopping had been completed for weeks. Going to the store tonight was not about shopping, rather it was about being in the middle of the Christmas crowd instead of being at home alone in the middle of my easy chair.

For no apparent reason and with no advance plan, I turned to the right and glanced at the display of best-selling current fiction books. This is the last category of books I would consider reading. Until every great book about history, government, education, Christianity and physical fitness have been read, plus some of the eternal classics of literature, I very rarely notice current fiction.

To my amazement, a life lesson was learned in the current fiction section. The reason was not a book. The reason was a dear friend who at that same moment was in the same section of the same store. Eye contact was quickly followed by a genuine hug of mutual fondness. Holiday greetings were shared. She was carrying two bags of wrapped Christmas gifts she had purchased at the store so she was obviously ready to leave, but she lingered to talk for a minute. Another hug was followed with this sincere statement, "God bless you" and she replied "you too."

How is that encounter a miracle? First, the lesser reason is the absolute lottery level odds against us being at the exact same place at the exact same time on that day. My schedule had included so many variables that arrival at the store could have been an hour earlier or an hour later. No doubt, her schedule had equal options.

The greater reason is that when we saw each other much more was seen than a friend to speak to or a dear person to say Merry Christmas to. What I saw was the possibility, the importance, the harmony, the goodness, the wonder of needing to share more time with family and friends. All of that can come from a moment of eye contact? Yes, it can if we are aware of, sensitive to, and responsive to the miraculous reality within that moment.

As I reflected upon our conversation, our hugs, our smiles, it was the initial face-to-face, mind-to-mind, heart-to-heart connection which happened that stood out. This human-to-human fulfillment was a blessing in my life because it revealed to me how essential it is for people to fully notice each other and appreciate each other.

How did this moment reveal so much? How did I know I was not making more of this than was true? Because we were given a gift of seeing each other and we added to the gift. It was not a hurried, "Good to see you. Sorry I have to rush off." It was "GREAT to see you!"

Notice more miracles. In some way it is miraculous that life exists, that the sun rises, and that a baby is born, that our brains think, that our hearts beat, that crops grow, that rescues occur, that kindness is shared, that thank you is said. In that perspective, all of life is a miracle.

In another way, the breakthrough insights, cures, joys, adventures, second chances, healed relationships, or given up on relationships restored; those are miracles.

Whether it be the smile of an infant connecting with parents, the smile of new friends, "I love you" or the next beat of your heart, notice more miracles and then give more thanks. Embrace family and friends and be thankful for those miracles.

41. GET OVER IT

In some circumstances and in some situations, "Get over it" is much more easily said than done. The doctor says "I'm sorry, we have done everything we can. I think it is a matter of days now." Family members do not get over that news instantly, quickly, easily and perhaps you never fully get over it although resilience enables you to not forever be controlled by grief, anger or despair.

As you drive in heavy traffic another motorist changes lanes quickly with no signal and comes close to hitting your car. No wreck. No injuries. Just lots of outrage. You will never be able to teach that person how to properly drive. You can turn to your 18-year-old son and 16-year-old daughter in the car with you and say, "That's an example of why I tell you that when you drive, you must assume that every other driver on the road is just about to do something very unwise and very unsafe."

You do get over the other person's carelessness as a driver. You also get over your anger at that person. You cannot control or impact their irresponsibility. You can prevent, minimize or resolve your anger. Get over it.

I was told to arrive at 12:40 p.m. to provide transportation to a funeral. I arrived precisely on time. 20 minutes later we drove off. My first thought was to resent being kept waiting. My second thought was that the sun was shining and the temperature was 50 degrees on a late December day. My third thought was that paying tribute and honoring a dear friend who had died should be done without any sign of resentment. I told myself to get over it–"it" being the tardiness of the person I was transporting.

I smiled, gazed at the bright blue sky and gave thanks that I had been reminded of what matters and what does not matter. We arrived at the funeral in plenty of time. Proper honor was expressed toward our lifetime friend whose faith, hope and love were the themes of the funeral. The funeral tribute said nothing of punctuality; rather, it emphasized faith, hope and love. I understood. Punctuality is proper, but faith, hope and love last forever.

The same funeral provided an unexpected answer to an unasked question. The answer emerged quite clearly and its clarity, power and certainty invited the question: When a loved one dies, how do friends help family members get over the death? First, death is not something that we ever get over with finality. The loved one is always missed and is forever remembered. Second, the difficulty of the funeral service is a challenge that the family must get through if not exactly get over. How do friends help the family members get through/over the funeral?

Hugs. Words are spoken. Memories are shared. Comforting thoughts are expressed. Offers of help are extended. Still, hugs prevail because some feelings cannot fit fully into words and because some degree of consolation for the heart, mind and soul can come only from an embrace. These hugs of consolation are no superficial arm to shoulder socialite hello, nor are these bear hugs with a bank vault grip. These are hugs of sincere, certain, pure concern, compassion, kindness and caring. A HUG, in this application, stands for Help Unload Grief.

42. BAKE MORE CAKES

Or cookies or pies or homemade bread or other traditional "like grandmother used to bake" kitchen treats.

Because they taste so good.

Because licking the icing off of the spoon is a priceless childhood joy.

Because the aroma throughout the house will be pure delight for everyone.

Because it's what parents and children have always done to share some wonderful moments together.

Because it's not mainly about the cakes, cookies, brownies, pies, rolls, biscuits or homemade bread. It's about the time together, it's about creating memories, it's about showing your children what you were taught by your mother or other relatives about cooking when you were a child, it's about being together.

There are many excuses which could explain why more cakes, cookies, pies or brownies are not baked at home in the kitchen with parent and child involved together:

- We're too busy
- It makes such a mess
- Our schedules just don't fit
- The bakery does it better
- It's cheaper to buy them at the mega-huge grocery superstore
- I don't have a good recipe
- What if they don't taste right?
- Everyone is off doing something on their own–we never get together to do anything.

Even if those excuses overlap with reality, they are unacceptable. For one family hour, turn off the television. Turn off the DVD, turn off the video game with in-your-face-graphics. Say no to phone calls, cell phones included. Turn off the computers. Get the homework and the exercise and the soccer practice and the errands completed earlier. Now, bake. How? Figure it out. Read the recipe information on the chocolate chip package. Use a cookbook. Use a recipe from an old recipe file your mother gave you on your wedding day. Try the cookie dough system the men used to bake cookies for that "Ladies night out" meal the gentlemen prepared for their wives in the neighborhood a few years ago.

There is never enough time for everything. There is always enough time for what we make most important.

In 15 years your 11-year-old, who will then be your 26-year-old when introducing you to your new grandchild, will not say "Remember that video game you got me when I was 11. It changed my life. I'll remember it forever." That 26-year-old could say "Remember that day we baked cookies and burned them so we put lots of icing on them and they still were awful so we tried to bake a cake and it was great, but the kitchen was a huge mess. I want to do things like that with my children."

In the too fast, too busy, grow up too soon pace of life, slow down and bake more cakes. It's not really about the cakes although they can be yummy. It's about the time with the people who help bake the cake. The cake will taste really good for several days. The memories of baking the cake will be delicious forever.

43. DRINK MORE WATER

The physical pain was much less than the emotional scar of embarrassment. The moments of magnificent victory were stolen by hours of unnecessary, but very real, loss. A few cups of water, maybe a quart, would have made all the difference.

For the first time in two years I ran five miles. The early morning sun streaked between impressionistic clouds with colorful bolts against the unblocked parts of the sky and against the light gray or white of the clouds. The temperature was a perfect 67. I had slept enough to awaken before the unkindness of the clock's shocking alarm. I had written a letter–the old fashioned type which is crafted by hand and energized by depth of reflection rather than speed of typing or speed of instant transmission.

Wait. Those five miles I ran might cause sore muscles. Let's clean up and go to the fitness club for a quick workout–hey, you could handle twice a day exercise 35 years ago in high school–and then relax those overused running muscles in the steam room. Better yet, let's help those certain-to-be sore otherwise muscles in the steam room and in the whirlpool.

After 10 minutes of steam and 10 minutes of whirlpool, my head felt light, my brain knew to take this warning seriously. I got out of the whirlpool soon, but not soon enough. I got to a bench and sat. Minimal relief. I know, a cool shower. I made it to the shower and soon fainted. A kind, worried person helped me up. I heard him ask "Are you ok?" I replied, "I think so". A bit dazed, I tried the shower again. Bad idea. I collapsed and missed the next minute or two. More kind people helped. The 911 call was responded to instantly. I was so embarrassed by it all.

Water. I begin drinking water. I remained still and drank more water. In 15 minutes I was much better. The rest of the day was given to serious contemplation of (1) What caused this? (2) How blessed I was that the cuts, abrasions and bruises are .01 percent of the awful damage that could result from two falls on hard shower stall floors and (3) what am I being told by this?

First, this was caused by my unnecessary error. Lesson learned. Typically, I act in smart, wise, intellectual, sensible, reasonable ways. Not after my five mile super run today. I love to run. A few years earlier my knees began to complain. I reduced running. Then my knees revolted. I quit running for a long time. Today, my knees were ready to go beyond the five miles I had worked up to, but I knew that gradual increases in miles is wise. At home after the run, I drank a little fluid, but did not seem thirsty. Wrong. My mistake.

Add little water replenished and the temperature of steam followed by whirlpool and you get 911 being called.

Second, death was possible if my body collapses and my head crashes to the floor. God almighty, thank you. And thanks for the people who helped me.

Third, lessons learned. I was not in the habit of eating breakfast. Plus, my work schedule forced a late lunch and a very late supper. Never again. Tomorrow I eat three proper meals. Tomorrow I drink water, water and more water. I'll avoid the steam room for a long time and probably never use steam or whirlpool on the day I run, or at least only after many hours of separation and much water.

There's more. This event shows interdependence. Total strangers rescued me. I'm accustomed to being the person who responds to and resolves a crisis. Lesson learned.

Plus, in the over 50 age group, much to my regret, some adjustments are needed. For right now, I'll go put some water in this determined-to-stay-young body.

44. PLAY MORE

Today I will play. The play will not be for the purpose of exercise or for the purpose of improving a skill. The play will be for the benefits of play. What will I play? Pool. I really enjoy shooting pool, so pardon me for a few minutes, please, while I go play pool.

I'm back. Here's what I noticed most about shooting pool, about play–it was calm. There was no pressure to move faster, work harder, finish early or endure stress. There was a peaceful pace. There was a sense of doing this just for the doing of it, with no pretense of more or less. I smiled at good shots and just kept trying after bad shots. It was good to play.

This is a good day to slow down and play because this is the day after my accident at the sports facility. It took me 30 minutes this morning to change all of my bandages. There are cuts on my right foot, both knees, my back, my left hand, my arms, and big abrasions on my hips. How did I manage to get so many cuts?

I've thought today that it is the cuts which are forcing me to change. The cuts will heal in a week or so. During that time I will have very limited physical activity. During that time I'll play more. During that time I'll implement changes that are long overdue. I ate a small supper last night and this morning for the first time in months, I ate breakfast. I also drank a bottle of water this morning. I did some work for classes I teach so our plans for the upcoming week are completed.

To me, taking a nap is in the play category. I'll take a nap this afternoon as the gentle rain which is falling now continues to create a lazy day.

I once asked a successful Hollywood movie producer why he was always so energized, so outgoing, so joyous, so full of life. He explained, "Our work is our hobby. We love what we do." For him, going to work is joyful because he loves what he does. He did not say that his work was play or was fun, rather his work is his hobby, his interests and talents applied to his career.

The fainting incident tells me to play more, to take more naps, to consider viewing my job, if possible, as if it is my hobby which may mean to change how I do the job or how I think about it because only a small part of my current duties and my attitude about those duties fit the hobby category. The work must be done, but how it is done could be revised in a healthy way.

During this day I'll also play with ideas, with thoughts, with concerns, with hopes, with evaluation of past failures and with plans for future successes. I will let my mind play and see what new mental adventures can soon become honorable results.

It is good to play more if you never play or rarely play. For this moment it is time for me to go to church. Worship is not play, but I can take the "love what I do" attitude to church with me today and do more than merely attend passively.

Today I will play more and tomorrow I will live, work, feel and think better for the playing done today. Work is not play. A job is not play. Yet perhaps taking the creative, energetic, joyous, refreshing attitude that is provided by today's play with me to work could be beneficial. It's worth a try.

45. ADMIT MORE DEFEATS

Consider these thoughts of a 34-year-old middle manager: "Success is impossible. I work harder, but it does no good. I work smarter, but it does no good. I offer my help to more people, but the offer is rejected each time. I complete my duties and I do more than is required, but it gets me nowhere. I apply for openings and I have more qualifications and experience than the person who gets selected. I ask people who I interviewed with to tell me what I need to improve, but they ignore my request or say "We needed to move in a different direction." I ask people who do not select me what skill or experience or qualification I need to acquire, but they give no answer." What does this mean?

One conclusion is that this will never change. It is sometimes necessary to admit that the only job your current employer will ever let you do is the job you have now which is the job you have had for too many years already. To admit defeat at this employer is the only way to experience victory because you have to go work somewhere else to be given the opportunity, the challenge and the responsibility you seek. It is in admitting this defeat that a new victory can become possible.

To stay where you are is to endure daily defeat. You were not made to endure permanent defeat. You have made the most of these years, but there is little or no benefit from adding another year to a job that is past diminishing returns and has become very unhealthy to continue. If this employer will not resolve the matter, another employer will. You are not necessarily called to work for a certain employer, but you are called to do a certain type of work. Where the call takes you, you eagerly and thankfully will go.

We are not taught how to lose, how to give up, how to admit defeat. We are taught to seek victory at all costs, to persist at all costs, to never admit defeat. Persistence can be beneficial, but blind. Unrealistic, rigid stubbornness can be destructive. Winning the permanent war can be done even if a temporary battle ends in defeat.

"But I know how to play T-ball, please don't make me bat against a pitcher or a pitching machine."

"But I've worked here for years. Sure it drives me crazy, but it pays the bills."

"Yes, we love each other, but we're comfortable being single and dating for three years has worked out fine. Why change? Marriage is risky."

Admit more defeats so you can open yourself to the pursuit of new victories. The new job will be an adjustment, but the old job is restricting, choking and going nowhere. Marriage brings new personal and interpersonal challenges, but its potential for goodness is unlimited.

If your status quo has limits, admit defeat and eagerly seek the next victorious adventure. There is no assurance that all will be well in the new endeavor but it could be very beneficial. There is a likelihood if your current status continues you may get nowhere as you increasingly dread each day, as you increasingly fade into insignificance and as you give up on who you really are and can be.

Notice how perfectly this verse from Psalm 23 applies: "He makes me lie down in green pastures." Sometimes we are made to lie down, to slow down, to reflect, to change, to be still, to be aware, to be wiser than before. Defeats can force us to do that and can help us prepare for the next victory.

Declare victory where you are by concluding that you have won all you can here. No more victories are possible there, only defeats. Pursue a better victory elsewhere.

46. BEYOND ALL I CAN ASK OR IMAGINE

In one week I had used four boxes of band aids. There were multiple cuts on my hands, arms, back, hips, knees and feet. Not since the years of skinned knees from bicycle wrecks had I been so banged up. The cuts healed so slowly at first. I wondered if being 50 years old was impacting me in worse ways than I had feared.

My body was still in slow motion. Falling had been frightening more than it had been an experience of physical destruction. Would I ever regain full fitness? This seemed more serious because 911 emergency personnel came to take care of me. I'm the person who resolves emergencies, not who causes emergencies. I was deep in doubt about ever reclaiming high levels of fitness for heart, mind, body and soul.

The week passed and healing finally seemed to accelerate. Still, one week after being injured, I had a pile of work to do at home that drained all remaining energy out of me. I was dead weight when I hit the bed Saturday night. I thought of what miserable company I would be for our family celebration of Mother's Day which would be tomorrow.

Sunday morning began with cool breezes entering my house. The unusual May heat of recent days would return mid-afternoon, but the gentle calm, soothing winds of the morning were joyous. I read passages from the Bible. I watered new sod in my yard. The sunrise was compelling. Dare I consider running?

Eight days ago my five mile run was part of the sequence which led to dehydration, overheating, fainting, injury and the 911 response. In prayer I asked for the courage to run. I dressed for running and that procedure told my body we are going to run. My mind accepted the instructions which the routine of preparing to run sent. I asked for and I imagined a four mile run. That would put me close to the achievement of eight days ago and would convince me that the week of no exercise had not done permanent, irreversible damage to my running hopes and goals.

The beauty of the sunrise was beyond what any artist could capture. There was a holy magnificence in creation this morning. I ran steadily with properly managed motion, stride and pace. The cool air was invigorating. The bottle of water at home would get my first attention when I returned–no dehydration this time.

After four miles, I knew that one more mile was possible. A 5th mile would be more than my prayer had asked or imagined, but stopping after four miles simply would offend the perfect harmony I knew my heart, soul, mind and body were experiencing.

As I approached the end of mile five, my courage, confidence and commitment increased. Let's go a few steps past five miles just to surpass the most recent run. A few steps grew into mile six. My body liked the idea. Heart, mind, body–especially legs–and soul harmoniously teamed up to complete the sixth mile.

This was the first time in two years I had completed a six mile run. Three years earlier my running reached a new level of accomplishment when I completed a mini-marathon of 13 miles. Two years earlier and last year my knees prohibited running more than two or three miles per workout. Eventually last summer I realized the knees were insisting on zero running. I switched to rowing, swimming, and every possible exercise machine at my health club that can give a workout that almost matches running– bicycle, treadmill, elliptical, hill climber and trendy infomercial types. For a runner, nothing can duplicate the experience of, the accomplishment of and the residual benefit of running.

There was no expectation that I could or would run six miles the week after a 911 category accident and a few months after taking much time off from running. Six miles was a distance that surpassed all I could ask for or imagine. I was blessed with a longer distance and a more wonderful experience than my mind could have asked for or imagined. The ramifications of and the possibilities of that conclusion are unlimited, for more miles that can be run and for more mileage in all areas of life.

Yes, I drank much water when I returned home. For achievements which are beyond all I can ask or imagine to actually happen, the lessons learned from earlier non-achievements must be applied.

Author's note: Ephesians 3:20 is the foundation for this essay.

47. LEARN FROM FAILURE

It was right there in front of me. I had hoped, worked, prayed and waited. It was right there in front of me. All I had to do was accept the offer and respond with equal eagerness. That never happened. For reasons such as fear, timidity, inexperience, stupidity, sin or selfishness, I did not embrace the moment, embrace the offer, embrace the possibility. I stayed within my comfort zone and, consequently, have been uncomfortable ever since.

Lesson learned. This time I have done all of the thinking and rethinking. This time I have anticipated all of the doubts and fears which will confront me. I have already disintegrated those doubts and fears. This time wisdom replaces stupidity. This time reaching out replaces selfishness. This time courage replaces fear. This time faith replaces timidity. This time knowledge replaces inexperience. This time, my answer is a potent, a powerful, a certain and an assured yes.

Life will never be the same nor should it be the same. For much too long failures of the past have choked possibilities in the present and have smothered hopes for the future. Not this time.

This time I have changed my methods, my approach and my thinking. This time I realize that there is more to lose by remaining in the status quo than by moving into the new endeavor. The assured tranquility of not changing is an illusion. That tranquility is a slow, but certain decline into merely going through the motions of being alive. Never again!

So offer that job, and my answer is yes. Agree with me that much more can and must be done and our answers will be the harmonious yes of unlimited achievement.

I have failed. I have failed repeatedly. Mistakes made. Opportunities rejected. I have caused those failures. I offer no excuse. I accept total blame. I also accept the challenge to apply what has been learned. The price of failure has been high, but it need not be permanent. I will invest that price into a radical revolution which touches the heart, mind, body and soul.

I was not born to fail, but birth of any human assures some encounters with and attacks of failure along the way.

The next time failure faces me, I will glare at it, march toward it, conquer it and give thanks.

The next time it will be different because the next time I will not be alone. New wisdom, new determination, new courage will accompany me. Failure temporarily defeated me. Failure is no match for renewed determination enlightened with new wisdom.

48. LEARN FROM SUCCESS

The graduate school students did work of a quality and of a quantity which surpassed all I had ever seen. How could the next graduate school class I would teach do better? There was a way. That way was within the prior success, but could occur only by making necessary changes to the prior success rather than merely repeating the actions of the earlier success.

So I made changes and the new success surpassed the old success. What were the changes and how were they made? I listened very, very closely to what the students were telling me. These people are capable and they are dedicated. Their career frustrations or difficulties are genuine. Their determination to do their job well is relentless. So I listened and then I provided ideas or experiences which enabled them to create solutions to their problems. They learned. They grew in confidence. They renewed their hope and commitment.

I learned also. By analyzing the causes of success insight was obtained about what had caused the success. In athletics, coaches and athletes are often heard to say after a loss that they will analyze their mistakes and make the necessary corrections. When a team wins a game, there is less analysis of what caused the victory than there would have been if the team had lost and thoroughly analyzed the reasons for the defeat.

Learn from success. Learn what caused the success. Identify the obstacles to the success and evaluate how those obstacles were overcome. Itemize the strengths which supported and enhanced success. How can those strengths be developed into maximum expertise? How can emerging strengths become more fully developed?

Do not let victory hide needed improvements. Winning does not mean you did your best. Analyze victory to find the path to a better victory, to a more challenging or difficult victory.

When a student makes great grades at school it can be beneficial to think with that student about what he or she is doing that is causing the success. When the student faces a new academic challenge, the insights about how success is caused can be applied and the process of evaluating what causes success can be used. When students who are doing poorly at school hear from successful students about how to achieve greatly, it can be revealing and inspiring for some students.

If a student who struggles with chemistry, but who is excellent in United States History class, can get advice and ideas from successful chemistry students it can be efficient and effective. The chemistry scholars do not do the work for their struggling friend; rather, they advise, guide, explain and encourage. The struggling chemistry student may realize that some of the skills and methods which enhance success in U.S. History class are skills and methods which can transfer to chemistry class.

Learning from success is sometimes limited because since success happened everything must be working fine. Wrong. Success can hide or cover-up possible improvements or flaws. Failure is often analyzed so lessons can be learned. Analysis of success can bring equally valid insights.

In Lexington, Kentucky, the local celebration of July 4th includes a 10 kilometer run called the Bluegrass 10,000. There are about 3,000 participants and very many additional kind souls who line the streets, yards and neighborhoods along the route to cheer for all of the runners.

I have two goals when I run in this July 4th event. First, my goal is to complete the entire distance. Second, my goal is to finish with a time equal to my age so at age 50 I hoped to complete the run in 50 minutes and 59 seconds. The first goal has always been reached. The second goal had not been reached yet until 2009, at age 55.

I do not declare loss because the winners of the race are a good 25 minutes ahead of me. I do not claim victory because 1,500 finish after me. Success is in having, in pursuing, in reaching my goals. The finish line is an illusion. The real goal is to take each of the 9,000 steps in the race well. There can be many small successes within each race, within each day, within each moment. At age 54 my finishing time in the race was 60 minutes and 15 seconds. The time was frustrating, but the finish line was reached. From this success I learned that the definition of success can change.

Still, I fully intend to run faster at age 55. This year's partial "success" taught me to work harder for next year's real success. I will train differently based on what worked or did not work this year. I will learn from success now to create a better success.

Did it work? Much to my amazement, yes. The training change was to run every other day instead of to run five or six times per week. Also, I cross-trained some and added tennis to the schedule.

The first mile was run in nine minutes 30 seconds in the July 4, 2009 race. That was much better than 11 minutes 6 seconds in 2008. I learned from the success of the first mile that beating an hour was very likely. At the end of the second mile the time was 18 minutes 20 seconds. I learned further that my training was sufficient and that the perfect weather of 68 gentle degrees, moderate humidity and partly cloudy skies was helping.

At the end of mile five the time was 46 minutes 6 seconds. If that pace is extrapolated the 55 minute goal could be narrowly missed. So it was time for an eight minute mile. Done. At the end of mile six the time was 54 minutes four seconds. The 6.2 mile finishing time was 55 minutes 21 seconds. The success of each mile in the race taught me that this could be the race of overall greater success.

It was encouraging to run my age. For that matter, given knee and other problems of recent years, it was encouraging to run at all. Now, what can I expect for future years? That will depend in part on how much I learn from this year's success and on how well that learning is applied.

49. WE ARE NOT OUR CAREER

We are much more than our career. Work is important. Work, our job, describes part of us, but it does not define all of us.

For many years I thought that I was my job and that my job was me. I have cherished my work usually. No occupation has touched my heart, mind and soul as being a teacher or a school administrator has. I have sought perfection in my work because it is attainable and because I have experienced it occasionally in moments, in classes, in ideas, in student progress and in memories relived. Still, life is more than my career and I am more than my career. I have to keep telling myself that over and over because it is contrary to my usual thinking.

Teaching is not merely what I do, teaching has been very much a part of who I am; however, the heart, soul and mind of a teacher function during the hours and days when school is not in session. Waking up on Saturday morning and putting life on hold for 48 hours until I can teach again on Monday would destroy two days of each week. Just doing school work during weekend days limits life. What is to be done? Sure, there are papers to grade and lessons to plan, but what else should one weekend include?

Live. Live more. Keep living. Quantity and quality are factors. Make the most of each moment. We measure life in years, but we live life in moments. Yesterday, a sunny Saturday, I attended a high school softball game. Some participants in the game once attended the middle school where I work. It was pure joy to visit with these dear friends of mine after the game. Those moments were filled with smiles and hugs. I was not a teacher in the classroom during those moments and the softball players were not students in classrooms, but our shared experiences in school had established a foundation for friendships. What happens if I do not attend that softball game? Life would have gone on, but without some smiles and hugs. Life is better with smiles and hugs.

I went from the softball game to visit my mother, who was recovering from shoulder replacement surgery. A dear friend of my mother, who is a nurse, is staying with mother full time for a week or two. How amazingly and wonderously saintly is that! She is donating her time and skills to care for my mother. Her nursing skills are superior. Her willingness to care is more vital. She is more than her career.

As I visited with my mother and her saintly nurse friend there were more smiles and hugs. My mother had left a voice mail message earlier in the day saying she was fine and that I need not come tonight. Had I not gone to visit, life would go on but without some smiles and hugs.

I have been fascinated by work in education. Perhaps I was born to be a teacher and a school administrator, but I was born to do more than that. I am expected to live a teacherly life which looks for ways to cause learning, to make a difference, to touch lives in classrooms, at softball games, at my mother's home and everywhere I go.

Maybe I am my career if I see my career as living fully 24 hours a day, each day with the heart, mind and soul of the teacher I am everywhere I go, in every moment I live, in every action I take. I see benefit in the idea of making life my career, rather than making my career my life; however, that will be a major change for me and the adjustment may come slowly.

This weekend shows that perhaps life can be lived with life itself as the ultimate career. These encounters show what might serve as transition for me. On Sunday a student of mine from 12 years ago–he was in high school classes I taught and he was on the high school soccer team I coached–saw me at a local tennis club. He instantly said with great joy and energy, "Dr. Babbage! I've quoted you three times in the last week. People at work kept complaining and I said 'Results not excuses' until they finally did the work."

A high school senior I know from his middle school years and I talked at the tennis club about his full scholarship to a nearby college. I attended a Sunday afternoon musical event where an 8th grader performed at a magnificent piano recital of 20 young musicians. I was captivated with each note played. Two high school students were in the youth Sunday Service at their church. I knew them during their middle school years and they keep in touch with me. I was thankful to be there to support their work.

Two high school juniors and I talked on Saturday at the YMCA. We met recently when I volunteered at a literary event at their school. Maybe I will get to be their teacher someday. So, this weekend was life enhanced by students from my career past, present and future. Life enhanced through career just might work if life and career are symbiotic.

Career is part of life. People are more than their career. This adjustment will take some getting used to for me, but it can be done. I can still be a good teacher or school administrator even if teaching or school administration are big parts of my life instead of being all of my life. Right? I think so. That has to be right. That just has to be adjusted to. This will take some work. For those of us who have always defined ourselves completely or mostly by our career, expanding the self-definition is not easy, but can be very meaningful. It needs to be done.

50. IMPOSE MORE DISCIPLINE

Burn up more calories than you consume. That is how weight loss happens. Select any diet plan, system, method, process, sequence or structure. Weight is lost when calories burned are greater than calories consumed.

Many parts of life have a similarly blunt and direct bottom line reality. For students who need to improve their grades at school, it is necessary to pay attention fully to teachers, do all homework completely and correctly, turn in all homework on time, study, ask questions, read, think, read more and keep reading, study more and keep studying.

For people who would like to change jobs, there are actions which must be taken to find, be considered for and get the desired job. For single people who seek to be married, there are actions which must be taken to find a proper, potential spouse. The phone will not ring with a magical announcement telling you, "You've won the ideal job, plus, you've won the perfect spouse."

My thoughts were of such blunt realities as I watched my weight increase by 10 percent during the winter months. This happens almost every year as the seasonal change eliminates outdoor activity, as the seasonal pace at my job increases and as the perpetual night–it's dark outside when I go to work and it's dark outside when I return home from work–imposes lethargy. By April I was sufficiently angry with myself to take the required actions. Some progress was made, but it was very limited. The weight gain stopped, but was not reversed.

What blunt, direct, disciplined action was needed? For me, there is only one exercise which during the past 30 years has been effective: run. The simplicity and the solitude of running appeal to me. The better fit of my clothes due to benefits of running regularly appeals to me. The enduring abundance of energy and of mental clarity which follow a good run appeal to me.

It was a Wednesday of glorious sunshine, warm temperature and clear skies. It was an irresistible call to run. I used a different route which took me through an attractive neighborhood where I would like to live, through the campus of a high school where I would like to work and along the sidewalk of a suburban residential area which borders tranquil farmland. For the first time in this spring season I ran for over an hour.

It's not as if running for 59 minutes is of little benefit and running for just a few minutes past one hour triples the benefits, but there is a multiplier effect which begins for me at the one hour mark. When I run for more than one hour I defy age, gravity, inertia, winter's weight gain and the other important requests for my time. I discipline myself to run over an hour because for me less than that is barely productive, is just maintaining, is just getting by. Over an hour is the promised land of progress, of adventure, of results and of joy. Each year it is more difficult for me to expand runs into the over an hour category; therefore, each year it is more important to improve the discipline on myself to run, albeit slowly, into the second hour. Then I drink much water.

When I impose this discipline upon myself, there are predictable barriers. The forces of evil on planet Earth seem to attack me with obstacles. I overcome that by doing what runners do–put on running clothes, stretch muscles and take the first step. Once I begin running the forces of evil have lost. The first step is the vital moment.

Along the way my mind might say, 45 minutes would be plenty today. I smile, veto that thought, run confidently and surpass 60 minutes. The process is simple: decide to run, prepare to run, start running, keep running, run more, declare victory and then drink ample water.

When that discipline is imposed often, there are many favorable results such as clothes fit better and physical fitness improves. There is another benefit which is the lovely reminder that to every problem, there is an equal and opposite solution. In many parts of life, as in running, deciding to take action, preparing for that action, beginning the action, continuing the action, completing the action and doing it all again soon will work.

If the body said stop, absolutely stop now after 45 minutes, that order must be obeyed. Discipline includes using good sense. Today the body had no complaints as minute 45 passed. I cooperated with my body and did what it allowed today–run over 60 minutes. It might not allow that on another day. Discipline includes limits. When the brain says run more and the body says you must stop, listen to the body's urgency and save the brain's dream for another day.

51. MAKE NO EXCUSES

Consider the following list of excuses:

- "I ran out of time."
- "I forgot."
- "I had something else to do."
- "I lost track of the time."
- "I meant to do that, but, you know, other stuff happened."
- "It wasn't my fault."
- "It just happened."
- "I kept putting it off. I never got to it."
- "Something else came up."
- "The delay was due to problems with a supplier. We did all we could."
- "The employees did not show up today. We can't finish your job."
- "It's too much work. I'll never get that done."
- "I was running late. Time just got away from me."
- "I know I owe you money. I'll pay you. Just not yet. There's a problem."
- "Prices have gone up. We can't change that. I have to charge you more than we agreed on."
- "Maybe next time. I'm too busy now."
- "Yeah, it's a pretty day, but I really don't feel like taking a walk. Maybe tomorrow."

The reader is asked to list additional common, unconvincing excuses:

-
-
-
-
-

Now, how can those excuses become results? What is the solution to "I forgot"? Write it down. Put a note where it will be seen. Leave a voice mail reminder message for yourself. Ask someone to remind you.

Please go through the list of excuses and think of ways that each excuse can be eliminated so more good results are achieved. The next essay will continue our thoughts about results.

52. GET MORE RESULTS

The day began with moments of joy and of hope. The moments stretched into minutes. The joy and hope stretched into certainty. The day was filled with reminders of a vision that rivaled reality, indeed, that needed to become reality.

When I dream during sleep the mental pictures usually form into a disjointed collection of unconnected, vague scenes. Not this time. The other people in this scene are real, very real. We were friends in high school. I last saw them 35 years ago, until this very recent, very vivid, very charming dream.

So, will I actually be in touch with them soon or did they represent other people, another idea? My mind tells me to find out. My heart tells me to build upon this dream to search its message and to secure its intended results. I do not see life as a mystical endeavor which sends us coded or mysterious messages. I see life as quite blunt. The dream felt more real than some reality. Life challenges me to make the scene in the dream or something better actually happen. Having been given a glorious glimpse of what could be, I am relentlessly determined to create that reality, to obtain that result. One question lingers and lingers.

How? One fact relentlessly remains–there is no simple answer to the how question. The dream was no preview of coming attractions. The dream was no call to exact action. The dream was a random intersection of nocturnal brain activities that merely teased me into hope, yet that hope is asking to be brought into the world as an actual result or, at least, is asking to be considered as a possible pursuit. Could I actually contact these people? Should I?

Life teased me again yesterday. Four former colleagues visited me at work. They updated me on their bold achievements of recent years. They are creating great results and greater futures. Life, why did you tease me yesterday with a glimpse of what I could have done only to have that fade into a mirage while I once again had to be face to face with that which would prefer to get rid of me only slightly less than I seek to be liberated of it?

Life does not answer my question. Life just laughs and goes on to tease another dreamer. Then life turns back at me and with a scornful look says, "You had your chances. How dare you ask for more? Of course, you could still reach new goals, but only if you get bold."

I know how to reply. I've studied life. I know life's debating tactics. "Ask for more. Never. Insist on more, demand more, work for more. Always."

Life smiles and says with a confident glow, "Close. Insist, demand and work are good, are vital. You need one more ingredient. You know what it is, so why wait."

I do know. I will not wait. Today I will begin a communication process with another person who can make happen what I cannot. Today, I accept that to reach my goals, I must secure the work of other people to open doors to which only they have the key. Today will be a time to get more results by doing my part which includes getting other people to do their unique parts.

One aspect of getting more results is to team up with more people. That can include people you have not teamed up with before. Find the most accomplished people, get their advice, become part of their team. Results await the people who work hard, work smart, think boldly and connect with very capable people.

53. REJECT MORE LIES

The pain in my neck was the first reality that I encountered on a Monday morning. There had been no pain the day before. What had changed? What had gone wrong? What needed to be done?

Applications of heat, use of common pain medication and use of heat wraps did some good, but did not solve the problem. Prescriptions provided by a very capable physician's assistant provided more relief and in a few days should correct this episode of neck pain; however, the pain will return. I would be living a lie to think that this pain is due to the one or two hours of exercise I get daily. I would be living a lie to think that the pain was due to sleeping in an improper position.

The pain is caused by other factors in life which would not previously be identified as reasons for pain. I know this to be true. I know that age is a factor. I know that this pain will return as long as I return daily to the same habits which could harm heart, mind, body and soul. Outsmarting age requires new tactics.

Life speaks the truth. Watching the sunrise or the sunset can be inspiring. Life speaks to us through such amazing presentations and reminds us of the truth that life has some amazing wonder, beauty, rhythm and majesty in it. Accepting and remembering such truth strengthens us to reject more lies.

The aging process is a challenge. Wear and tear take a toll. We cannot reject the fact that older bodies feel new pains which never were there before. There are some solutions or partial solutions. I will not lie to myself about the impact of wear and tear, nor will I give that impact any more power than the absolute minimum of reality.

Some pain in life has a physical beginning or cause and a physical conclusion or cure. Some other pains are explained differently. It would be a lie to conclude that my current pain is purely physical in cause and cure. Maybe my neck hurts because my heart aches and my soul is restless.

The true cure for this pain begins with rejecting the lies that would distort the true cause of the pain and the true cure of the pain. Maybe I need a different pillow. Maybe I need a new hobby. Maybe I need both.

When we reject all lies we are face-to-face with life's truth, face-to-face with our soul, face-to-face with life, face-to-face with God. Life is better lived with such face-to-face courage and conviction. Confronting lies, rejecting lies is a healthy process. Embracing truth is even healthier.

54. BREATHE DEEPLY MORE

What? Breathe deeply? How does that action fit in with every other idea in this book? It is one more way to enhance life. Several exercise experts, nutrition advisors, massage therapy trainers and public health leaders have mentioned to me that people do not always breathe correctly. How is that possible? We do not decide how to take each breath, it just happens automatically, similar to each beat of the heart.

Or does it?

When the physician tells us to take a deep breath, we take a deep breath. There is no identical process for the instruction "take a few slower heart beats." So, how are we supposed to breathe? You will need to ask an expert about the how part, but we can consider the why.

What happens when a person takes a few deep breaths? Often there is some tranquility that comes with the change in breathing pace. The busy pace of life may have been matched with a busy pace of breathing. The fast pace of life prevents a deep awareness of each moment. The fast pace of breathing prevents a deep intake of air and more effective release of air.

Breathe deeply more. While standing in line to check out at the grocery store, breathe deeply. While waiting in traffic for the light to change, breathe deeply. While enduring another extended time on hold or listening to the annoying list of menu options the automatic answering system is listing, breathe deeply. While in church, breathe deeply. While the busy pace of life crowds in, breathe deeply.

While writing this essay I have paused a few times to breathe deeply. The results always amaze me because deep breaths usually are so simple to give to yourself. I always sense new calm, new peace and new tranquility amid the deep breaths. Then I return to normal breathing, but with a new appreciation of and a new reminder for occasionally deeply breathing.

I doubt that deep breathing will emerge as a cure-all which eliminates illnesses that defy remedy. I doubt that the $49.95 infomercial product which offers an at-home deep breathing kit of trinkets is worth a penny. I doubt that lives will be forever changed because of a few deep breaths.

Yet, occasional moments can be enhanced if we fill our lungs patiently and fill those moments with the calm of deeper breathing. A life, a day–both are composed of moments. Take a few moments now to take a few deep breaths. Notice the price tag–no charge at all.

55. BEGIN MORE CONVERSATIONS

"How is this job working out for you?" I sincerely asked the teenager who was working at the check-out line in the grocery store where I shop regularly.

"Oh, it's not bad. It's a job. Some of my friends from school work here. So that makes it better."

The mention of school intrigued me. "Where do you go to school?"

"I'm a senior at James Madison High School. I'm really eager to graduate. Do you work at a school?"

I explained that I was a middle school assistant principal, but that I also taught one class daily–8th grade Economics. He then asked me what color of ink I use when I grade papers. I gave the common answer of "red" and he then gave me advice that I have followed for years.

"Try using green. It stands out just as much as red, but green is a friendlier color. Students are more likely to read what you write on their papers if you use green ink."

"Thanks for the great idea. I'll use green from now on."

That conversation did not have to occur. I could have silently moved through the check-out lane while the clerk silently processed my grocery items. We were not required to speak, but by conversing there was nothing to lose and possibly something to gain. As it turned out, I did get a very good idea which I have used ever since.

Even without getting a great idea, the conversation was worth the effort to bring a moment of interaction into the otherwise ordinary moment of checking out at the grocery store.

Begin more conversations. Of course, there is wisdom in being somewhat selective. Do not be rude as you begin a conversation. When the preacher is in the middle of the sermon do not ask a person sitting near you for a suggestion of a good restaurant to go to for lunch after church. Do not violate common sense rules of manners, safety or of sensible precautions.

For years my house has been treated monthly to prevent insects. The same company has provided this pest service for 19 years. The technicians who have come have always been polite and conscientious, plus they have been very friendly. We have had very enjoyable conversations. No doubt, they could do their job at my home in silence and I could merely hand them a check when their work was completed. Instead, we talk about politics, sports, topics in the news and, if necessary, insects. I rarely see a bug in my house, so the pest control plan is working. I always have a good conversation with the pest control technician, so the friendly discussion plan is working also.

I once owned a small house that had a big front porch. My next door neighbors and I had many front porch conversations as they sat in the comfortable, traditional front porch swing and I sat on the ledge at the end of my porch. The house I live in now has no front or back porch. No house on my street has a front porch. Modern houses seem to have been built for isolation instead of interaction. Why is that the current preference? What does that architecture style tell us about ourselves?

A neighbor was in her front yard last weekend. I walked over and we talked about several topics including schools, jobs, summer yard work. We smiled several times and laughed occasionally. That conversation was optional, but was quite delightful.

Begin more conversations. Text messaging does not count. Very short cell phone chats do not count: "How are you?" "I'm ok. How are you?" "I'm ok. See ya later." Points are given only for face-to-face multi-paragraph conversations in which you listen as much or more than you talk.

56. TEACH YOUR HERITAGE

Robert Johnson was a preacher in Western Kentucky. To be more precise, Rev. Johnson was a Methodist circuit riding pastor in and around Lyon County, Kentucky in the late 1800s and early 1900s. Rev. Johnson was my great-grandfather; however, we never met. He died long before I was born so our introduction will occur in heaven and we will have eternity to get well acquainted.

Although I do not know my great-grandfather, I do know much about him. My grandfather, Keen Johnson, taught me about our heritage. I know that family life in the home of a 1900 era Methodist circuit riding preacher was highly disciplined. My grandfather attended church all day on Sunday and always attended Wednesday evening prayer services. My grandfather was often the only child or teenager at the Wednesday evening service, but his attendance was mandatory.

I also know that life for my grandfather as he grew up in the loving, disciplined home of a Methodist circuit riding pastor was life on a very limited budget. My grandfather's greatest desire as a child was to have a bicycle, but his family emphasized faith over finances and no bicycle could be afforded. I cherish the memory of my grandfather's smile as he presented my brother and me each with a new bicycle when we were nine and six years old. We loved those bicycles. Our grandfather loved giving them to us even more.

Robert Johnson often told his son, Keen Johnson, that the day would come when Keen Johnson became governor of Kentucky. My grandfather deeply appreciated his father's encouragement, confidence, guidance, wisdom and fatherly love, but the career achievement of governor seemed a distant impossibility for a young man growing up in a humble home.

In 1939 Keen Johnson was elected governor of Kentucky. His only disappointment was that his father and mother did not live to see that event. I'm certain that they watched closely from heaven.

It was a difficult time to be the governor of any state. The Great Depression continued, World War II was brewing and then the

U.S. entered the war in 1941. Still, when Keen Johnson became governor of Kentucky, the state was in debt. When his term as governor ended, the Commonwealth of Kentucky had a financial surplus. Governor Johnson learned how to manage money in that humble, holy home where his parents taught him abundant faith and frugal finances.

My grandfather and I had many wonderful conversations. My favorite discussion with him was about my career interest in teaching. He was so pleased, so supportive and so encouraging.

When I completed my doctorate my only disappointment was that my grandfather had not lived to see that happen.

I have some pictures of my great-grandparents. I have many pictures of my grandparents and parents. The next generation in our family loves to hear the stories which go with those pictures. An individual's life span is limited. A family can live forever through the generations. Teach your heritage to your children. It is their heritage also. It is the gift of earlier generations to future generations, but the gift comes through you.

57. DEMAND EXCELLENCE

First of self and then of others. During the years I have taught high school or middle school, my work weeks averaged 70–80 hours during the school year. Evenings and weekends were filled with lessons to plan, studying to do and papers to grade. Some friends and some family members occasionally asked me if those hours could be reduced. There probably were some efficiencies available, but I chose to be 100 percent thorough which required excessive time commitment.

There were always two very important benefits to that standard of excellence. One, my conscience was clear knowing that I had done everything possible to effectively teach. Two, my work ethic was contagious and some students expected more from themselves than the mere "good enough" level because Dr. Babbage's effort inspired them.

Demand excellence also means to acknowledge and to appreciate excellence. I called the local cable television company last week for some repair work. We discussed the problems and scheduled the service call. The technician was exactly on time, was polite, solved the problems and then made other improvements when he noticed some old equipment that needed to be replaced. I called his employer and reported his excellent work. We get more of what we reward, plus, the gentleman deserved the recognition.

During my decades as an educator it has always amazed me that schools have such extraordinary results in sports, with marching bands and with other activities. Coaches do not end basketball practices with the last shot having been missed. They run the play or the drill until the shot is made. Marching band directors do not end rehearsal with the wrong notes played or the wrong steps taken. The band practices up to and beyond the level of excellence. Excellent results occur where and when excellence is demanded.

One of my favorite students sets the standard for being completely prepared for class, for being totally attentive and involved during class and for completing all class assignments on time. What inspires her work ethic? She has no toleration for anything less than the best she can do. What does she demand of herself? Excellence.

Demand excellence politely, but emphatically. When a company that has provided service to me for 20 years delayed and delayed with one project, I wondered what had happened to their previous standard of punctual, accurate, cordial service. I sent them an old-fashioned letter and asked the question, "You have always provided expert service. Is something wrong? I just don't see why this is taking so long. Let's resolve this, please, by next Monday." It was resolved before next Monday. I would like to think that one reason for the quick action was that I had reminded them of how good they are.

It is similar to when I comment to a student who makes some mistakes "You are better than that." No student has even replied to me, "Actually I'm a lot worse than that." The response is usually a contrite silence or a statement similar to, "Yeah, I know, I don't know what I was thinking."

Demand excellence. Exemplify excellence. Acknowledge excellence. Excellence is often a function of how you think and how you work, not of income or social status or fame. Excellence is available to everyone who thinks excellently, works excellently and lives excellently. Demand excellence of yourself and of others. Be, live, think, do that which is excellent.

58. CHASE MORE BUTTERFLIES

OK. Leave the innocent butterflies alone to explore nature without being chased. There is no reason to aggravate the butterflies or the animal rights advocacy groups which oppose butterfly stalking, chasing or disturbance of any type.

Still, chase more conceptual butterflies in the artistic, imaginative, creative, wondrous way that a child would be intrigued by an actual butterfly. Chase the career dream that was abandoned years ago, but which still visits your mind, your heart and your soul when you think about what might have been, and then update that thought to what still could be.

Chase the promise you made to yourself to feed the hungry, to participate with a church group that visits inmates in prison, to volunteer at a nursing home reading to residents who long for a visitor, to help coach a Special Olympics event, to mentor a troubled teenager, to shovel the snow or cut the grass for a senior citizen neighbor, to help a friend who runs for public office, to write notes of encouragement to friends who face difficulties, to help a person who is blind safely cross the street.

To be honest, there are reasons to have grave concerns about the United States of America. Our national government has imposed certain financial weakness on itself and on this country through decades of irresponsible borrowing, deficits, debt and unaffordable promises. This nation's financial integrity, trustworthiness, and international standing have been compromised. We yearn for national leadership which will restore wisdom, competence, discipline, honor and common sense to our national government and to our republic, but no such leadership emerges.

In the absence of competent national leadership, the citizens will need to lead the way in the local area which they can touch.

Chase the butterfly in your neighborhood by being part of, or starting, neighborhood cook-outs and other gatherings on your street.

Chase the butterfly in your school district by volunteering to assist at a school. Chase the butterfly in your city by volunteering time to get leftover food from bakeries, restaurants and grocery stores distributed to food banks or homeless shelters.

Perhaps we need to borrow a perspective from colonists who established settlements along the Atlantic coast in the 1600s. The work which was done, those colonists did themselves. There was an honorable, vital emphasis on family, community, church, shared effort and mutual obligation. That emphasis could serve a purpose now.

Chase more butterflies, not with an actual sprint toward a colorful flying natural wonder, but directly to a person who may simply need a moment of your time to remove them from the limitations, almost like a cocoon, in which life has wrapped them.

Your effort can release their butterfly within. Chase that butterfly and you release some of your goodness.

59. THANK MORE PEOPLE

Thank you.

Thanks very much.

I appreciate your help.

Thanks. I could not do that without you.

Thanks for calling.

Thanks for being here.

Thank you for the best birthday party ever.

Thank you for being the best teacher I ever had.

Thanks for listening to me.

Thanks for letting me do that. It was so important to me.

Thanks for your concern.

There are opportunities each day to say thank you, to e-mail some words of appreciation. To actually write and mail a thank you note.

One thought of editorial comment–when children or teenagers are misbehaving and finally comply with your instruction to stop the misbehavior, saying thank you is not needed. "Quit hitting each other. Quit. Quit right now. I don't care if you were just playing. Do not hit each other. Thank you." That thank you is a non sequitur.

A genuine, sincere thank you logically follows a beneficial action. "Thank you for getting your room cleaned up without having to hear any reminder." "Thank you for fixing my favorite supper." "Thank you for going to the hospital with me. Those tests were difficult to go through. I really needed you." "Thanks for running those errands for me."

If you do something beneficial for someone and they do not say, write or communicate in any way the appreciation you deserve, keep doing actions which are beneficial to people anyway. Being kind, helpful, caring and supportive have inherent benefits. If the person you were kind to does not say thanks, listen to the peaceful assurance in your heart, soul, and conscience telling you that your kind action was right and was important. That assurance is life itself saying thank you. Thank you for reading this book.

60. WALK THE DOG

Why? Because every step a dog takes on every walk is filled with the dog's total fascination about every tiny bit of life that is encountered. The path that to a human walking alone is ordinary, mundane, worthless, generic and a waste of time is to a dog, priceless, wonderful, lovely, intriguing, to be fully explored and to be fully appreciated. Sometimes people need to see life from a dog's point of view.

We use the exact same path for every walk, but it never seems to be a re-run. When I drive up to the front of the house where my brother, sister-in-law and their children live, the dog comes to the door and begins a ceremony of pure rejoicing. He jumps, dances, spins, wags his tail, sings and smiles because he knows that we will take a walk. I always take the dog, Rudy, for a walk. He benefits from the exercise. I benefit from watching him find new adventure along the same old path.

Trees, bushes, blades of grass, plants, scents, sounds, breezes, raindrops, snowflakes, sunshine–the dog is fascinated by it all, loves to jump right into it all and refuses to miss anything. He sees much more in those two blocks than I notice. There is a vital lesson in that canine perspective.

We have been down this path before, but that does not make today's journey along the path any less magnificent than the first journey was. We get to go together along the path again, right here, right now. What could be better? Who needs to go anywhere else? Why go anywhere else? There is more to explore right here than we could ever completely explore.

Rudy can walk around his yard alone. The high technology system and the very effective training in his puppy year combine to keep him in or near the yard. He can walk alone, wander alone and run alone in the yard.

Rudy would much rather go for a walk even though that means he is connected to the leash. What minimal limitation the leash imposes the unlimited wonders encountered during a walk greatly surpass. Plus, he really likes to be with a person. He just knows that experiences shared are better than experiences done alone.

Rudy's perspective on taking a walk is a very healthy perspective on how to live each day. Explore anew, encounter anew, look again, appreciate again, experience all there is to experience right here, right now.

Rudy does not know if he will get to take a walk tomorrow. He does know that he is taking a walk right now and he sure does know how to get the most out of now. Putting all we have into now and getting the most we can out of now, that's what Rudy reminds me of every time we take a walk.

Everything else can wait. Every excuse is unacceptable. Now is calling. Rudy and now and a walk. Some joys in life are available only right here, right now.

61. HUG MORE OFTEN

My mother thrived on hugs. She liked chocolate candy and she liked almost any flavor of ice cream, but health concerns made those pleasures off limits, usually. She enjoyed listening to the radio, she delighted in visits with her grandchildren; however, she thrived on hugs. If given the choice of being allowed to have chocolate again or the hug of a grandchild, chocolate would get no votes.

Although it became laborious for my mother to lift herself out of her automated chair, she would make that effort for "one more hug." If I stayed for a few more minutes I would again hear her genuine request for "one more hug." I noticed that my mother and her dearest friends greeted each other with a gentle hug. Arthritis, shoulder surgeries, other aches and pains were forgotten as arms reach out and friendship was affirmed.

When I arrived at my mother's retirement community apartment with the groceries, I was eager to put the food in its proper place. "I haven't had a hug yet" was often heard if I lingered with the groceries.

A student whom I taught in high school in 1992 and I saw each other a few years ago for the first time in about 15 years. Human beings rarely smile as we smiled upon that grand reunion. She hugged me with such pure energy and honest emotion that I finally understood why hugs mean so much to people. One reason is that when a person really hugs you they are totally concentrating on you yet it is in a socially acceptable way. How often do we get the undivided attention of another person? How often do we give our undivided attention to someone else?

The staged hugs at televised awards show events are not what I have in mind. Those "air hugs" are just one more prop in the show.

"I now pronounce you husband and wife" hugs also are not the idea. That embrace is a unique aspect of a 'til death do us part linkage.

The trendy hugs of a generation which denies itself disciplined, polite greetings in search of a hug thrill, are also not the intention.

Hugs–reaching out, connecting, more than a handshake, less than a caress. An expression of friendship, thanks, commitment, perhaps love. A way to say that you matter to me in a way that I can express only through an action on my part and a reciprocal action on your part that for a few moments means we totally concentrate on each other.

Do not hug total strangers. Do not hug people who prefer to shake hands only. Respect the other person's comfort level.

Do hug when the moment says this is a time to hug. That moment cannot be recovered if you let it pass by. Be polite, be tactful, be genuine. Family members hug each other differently than friends hug each other. Married couples hug each other differently than acquaintances do. Colleagues could hug to celebrate a major business achievement and that is similar to athletes hugging to celebrate a victory.

Hugs can also be acts of sympathy and consolation. A dear friend and I hugged at great length while we both cried at a funeral home. That hug was to comfort, to assure, to grieve together.

When the time is right, when the reason is true, when both of you are obviously in agreement, hug that other person. Some of those moments just happen, so be ready. Some of those moments are made, so get busy.

62. EAT MORE ICE CREAM

It meant a lot to my students. Typically I will do anything that is G-rated, legal and ethical to enhance the education of my students. This time, their request passed my requirement and surpassed their hopes.

From time to time I used to bring treats for my students. Middle school students always liked cookies, candy or fresh fruit. High school students have liked cookies, nutritious cereal bars or bubble gum. The other favorite has been homemade granola bars which I make.

Today was different. A student had commented recently that having ice cream in class would be ideal. How do I conveniently serve ice cream to a classroom full of high school students? The answer was to get a box of bite-size, chocolate covered ice cream goodies. When I brought those treats to class the smiles were instant confirmation that this was the right choice.

The students know that I am very particular about what I eat. My favorite food is plain yogurt. Their expressions when they hear of plain yogurt are the looks that follow the consumption of the worst tasting medicine of all time.

There was one ice cream bite-size treat left. "Dr. Babbage, that one is for you. You have to eat it." I did have to eat it because this was a shared experience of teacher and students. Yes, the ice cream was yummy.

A few months later I stopped at a local ice cream store to get a gift card for a friend. One of my students from that same class works at that shop and was there on the day I shopped for the gift card. After the card was purchased, she politely said the inevitable, "Dr. Babbage, you have to taste our ice cream." I asked for her recommendation of a flavor. "Cookie dough" she said with absolute certainty. It was so good.

"That's twice in the same year I've had ice cream" I commented to the young scholar. She smiled, said, "I know" and seemed to be very eager to tell her friends the good news.

There are times and places where the only right action to take is to eat ice cream. Of course, we need our fruits, vegetables, whole grains, dairy products and protein daily. We need to exercise daily. We just might also benefit from an occasional taste of ice cream. Just like my mother on those holidays when she got to violate the ice cream prohibition.

On my older nephew's second birthday he was having great fun eating a bowl of ice cream. He got to the part where the melted ice cream and a spoon just were not a good match. He picked up the bowl and covered his face with the remainder of the melted ice cream. Nothing was left in the bowl. He declared victory. He showed us how to eat ice cream. We still laugh at the picture of his head disappearing into that bowl.

Eat more ice cream. I once worked for an advertising agency and one of our clients was a large dairy products company. I visited their manufacturing facility where they made ice cream. Tasting that high quality product as it left the production line before entering the freezer was to taste the equivalent of old-fashioned, hand-cranked, hot summer day ice cream. Twenty-four years later I can vividly and precisely remember that flavor. There is only one conclusion–eat more ice cream. Not all day, every day. Not instead of fruits and vegetables.

Some moments just require ice cream or go better with ice cream. Sometimes ice cream makes the moment. Who knows– maybe you could create an ice cream moment with friends or family today. Yes, I still prefer plain yogurt, but there are ice cream moments which are among the charming parts of life.

63. ASK MORE QUESTIONS

The Sunday School teacher was concerned that her students were not asking questions. The Bible verses had been read. The learning activities had been completed. Still, the teacher expected some questions from the middle school students. She tried one more time. "So now that we have heard a lot about God, who has a question? Think of it this way. If you could ask God a question, what would you ask?"

That intrigued one student who said, "I understand that in the beginning God created the Heavens and the Earth. I mean, I still wonder where was God before the beginning and what was God doing, you know before the beginning stuff." The teacher was amazed. Another student added, "Yeah, that would be so cool to know. What was God doing before, I guess, before everything else began?" The discussion that followed was so lively that the topic eventually became the emphasis of a sermon preached by the pastor of that church. One question can ignite some profound thinking.

Ask more questions. Before you spend money ask yourself if some or all of the money could be saved. Is this potential purchase really necessary? Is there a way to legally purchase the item at a lower price?

Before you drive in the car to run some errands, ask yourself about the most efficient route to take so you save time and gasoline. Ask yourself also if you could "walk the errands" instead of driving everywhere. Maybe the destinations are close enough that you could park the car in one central spot and walk to all of the errand locations.

When you buy a car, do much research and ask many, many questions. You and the person you are seriously dating have some questions to ask each other. The employer you have always wanted to work for may be impressed if you ask questions about job possibilities. People who do interview you for a job expect you to have some impressive questions for them as part of the interviewing process.

Citizens of the United States should ask governmental leaders some serious questions such as "Social Security needs to be adjusted. The system as it is set up now cannot be sustained. What changes do you recommend?" "The national debt is continuously increasing and is out of control. How can you help solve this problem?"

Parents and guardians need to ask their children or teenagers serious questions about friends, school, tobacco, drugs, alcohol, bullying, automobile safety, career ambitions, part-time jobs, family rules, social media and other topics vital to the growing-up years.

Parents and guardians will benefit by creating the home atmosphere in which children and teenagers are comfortable asking questions from the simple, "Could we have pizza for supper tonight?" to the more complex, "Could I go to a party tonight?" and then to the very challenging–"I need a car. How can I get my own car?"

"The service you will do to check why my internet connection is inconsistent is done at no cost to me, is that correct?" The answer I was given confirmed that there would be no cost. The technician did superior work. I called the company to compliment the employee. I hope that his supervisor asked him what he did to provide such good service–prompt, polite, professional work–so every employee can be reminded of those very effective characteristics.

Ask more questions, then take a few moments to pause and to reflect on the answers you were given. Those answers might be sufficient or they could inspire you to ask more questions.

64. CHERISH MORE MOMENTS

It was about 7:30 a.m. on a Tuesday in early May. The school where I was teaching then began first period class at 8:30 a.m., so this student was quite ahead of schedule. I cordially greeted him and then I heard him say some very lovely words.

"I got in. I was accepted into the program. Thank you so much for the letter you sent. I know that it helped a lot."

Rejoice and give thanks. About two weeks earlier he had asked me for a letter of recommendation which he needed immediately. It was an honor to write it. Now he was telling me the great news of his acceptance into a summer academic program at a college in another state. There are about 200 applicants of whom 35 are selected. It was a joyous moment when this young scholar told me the good news. I congratulated him and I cheered. It was a moment to cherish. It is a moment I still cherish.

Two days before my father died, I was with him for a long time in the hospital. He could hear me and he could understand me. He was attentive but he was deathly ill. I updated him on all of the summer activities his grandchildren were involved in that week. We talked about church and politics. His lunch arrived and I tried to offer him food. He politely refused to eat. A nurse told me later that people who are near death have no interest in eating.

"I love you a lot Dad," were my final words to my father. "Love you lots," were his last words to me. I cherish that moment. I am thankful that my father and I said to each other the words that matter more than any others.

"Dr. Babbage, Congratulations." When I heard those words in May 1993 from the chairman of my doctoral committee I thanked God, smiled and cherished that long anticipated moment. The years of relentless effort had been completely worth it.

I was eight years old. Christmas was being celebrated at my dear grandparents' home in Richmond, Kentucky. Their home was pure Americana. The dining room setting was pure Norman

Rockwell. We had gathered to affirm the love within our family and to give thanks for the love of God.

My grandfather, an absolutely perfect gentleman, handed my grandmother, a lady of unsurpassed goodness, a Christmas present. She opened it and began crying. I asked my mother, "Doesn't she like her present?" Mom explained that my grandmother liked the gift more than words could express. Tears from a devoted wife to her death-do-us-part devoted husband created a moment to cherish.

I had walked 430 miles from St. Louis, Missouri to Cincinnati, Ohio. It was a thrilling excursion, a fantastic workout and two weeks of moments to cherish. The walk was to promote a March of Dimes walkathon which would be held a few weeks after my return to Cincinnati.

Upon arrival in Cincinnati, I walked to the Cincinnati Reds baseball stadium and handed the baseball I carried from St. Louis to the Cincinnati March of Dimes poster child. Baseballs used then by major league teams were made by a sporting goods company which was headquartered in St. Louis.

God bless him, that smiling boy in his Cincinnati Reds uniform took the baseball from me and threw it right into the glove of the Cincinnati Reds catcher. The crowd cheered. The boy and his parents grinned. I smiled and cherished that moment.

The sunrise was majestic. The air was crisp. The sky was clear. A few birds sang. It was one of many, many mornings which began with an invitation from life to cherish the moment. Despite the perspective that something unusual must occur to create a moment to cherish, this time of pure tranquility was filled with reasons to cherish the moment.

Cherish more moments, some of which you create and others you just receive and embrace.

65. LISTEN MORE

To children.
To preachers.
To friends.
To family.
To nature.
To conscience.
To spouse.
To wisdom.
To truth.
To grandparents.
To God.
To classical music.
To the old, old hymns of the faith.
To your spouse again.
To scripture lessons.
With total attention.
With heart, mind, body and soul.
With purpose.
With sincerity.
With no intentions of speaking soon.
Really listen and hear and understand and know. Listen:
To the relaxing, inspiring sounds of ocean waves.

To the music created by birds who sing their appreciation of another new, unexplored day.

To criticism, whether offered with a loving motive or a vindictive motive. Listen to the criticism and extract its truth.

To encouragement which could motivate you to become more than you would otherwise consider becoming.

To yourself.

To advice you were given years ago, perhaps when you were a child or teenager, but which still is applicable.

To people who completely disagree with your ideas. Why? Because truth emerges when ideas collide.

Listen. Listen more. Keep listening.

Of course, listening needs to be followed by making decisions and taking actions. After making decisions, keep listening. After taking actions, keep listening.

Listen to wise people whose lives confirm that they have gained extraordinary insights.

Listen to people who have learned lessons through overcoming obstacles.

Listen to people who have succeeded in endeavors in which you seek to succeed.

Listen to people who work in careers which are of interest to you.

Listen to people who have failed, have persisted, have tried again and have endured.

Listen to the wisdom which is found in great works of literature, of biography, of history, of science, of philosophy, of theology, of government and of other topics of interest to you.

Listen to that which is wholesome, G-rated, legal and ethical. There is no reason to listen to vulgarity, immorality, illegality or unethical trash. There is no delete function in our memory, so listen, but be alert to and selective about what you hear.

Listen more and listen more carefully.

66. BE AND BECOME

Over 30 years ago a professor at my college and I debated whether the four years of college were intended as a time for a student to "be" or to "become". As lofty as that question may seem, our debate was very serious and quite practical.

He contended that college was that unique time in life when a person could genuinely be a person with no pretense, no illusions, no mortgage and no demands placed on you which were more substantial than the demands you decided to place on yourself or to avoid placing on yourself.

I insisted that the purpose of college was to provide a new foundation upon which a student could build toward the person he or she was to become. My thought was that each college class, each college experience and each college failure or success was part of you becoming the person you could become, was part of you living the life you should live then and now.

I still favor the become idea. To be implies to stand still as you exist. To become implies to continually seek improvement, challenge, growth, new meaning and new ways to make a difference.

Extrapolate that college debate from the four years between ages 18 to 22 and think of the totality of life. Are we on this planet to be or to become, to exist or to thrive, to wander or to advance, to simply notice or to meaningfully experience that which is purposeful as a part of a continuous sequence of becoming, becoming more, becoming better?

Sure, being fully alive in and aware of each moment is healthy. Moments connect with other moments to become the full life we live. Making each moment count means that the combined moments will count more abundantly and become more meaningful.

I do everything possible that is g-rated, legal and ethical to be a good teacher; however, each day at school I enter the building expecting myself to become a better teacher that day than I have been before.

This is more than semantics. This is more than a different form of a complex verb. This is an idea. The word be is included in the word become, so that is interesting linguistically. The idea of become builds on the current moment of being, so that is of greater importance.

Become. Become more. Keep becoming. There is a vitality, a dynamism, an emergence that become includes that be does not necessarily include. Part of my understanding of being is that I am always expected to become better.

Maybe the limits which are expressed in the statement "I'm only a human being" can be surpassed with the statement "I am a human becoming more and better than ever." Which sounds more adventurous and compelling–"I am a human being" or "I am a human being who is becoming whole, complete and total?"

67. RESPOND TO MORE NEEDS

What would it take for hunger to be eliminated? Part of the solution to the problem of hunger would be for enough people who have ample food to take action to help people who have insufficient food. On a planet where some people desperately need to lose weight and other people desperately need to eat; the issue does not seem to be the worldwide supply of food. The issue seems to be that some people have access to more food than they need while other people do not have access to adequate food.

How complicated would it be for nations of the world, churches throughout the world, people throughout the world to team up and eliminate hunger? Would it be more difficult than it was for the 13 colonies to establish their independence? Would it be more difficult than it was to successfully fight World War II? Would it be more difficult than it was to travel to the moon and back? Mankind has completed tasks which were equally demanding as, or more demanding than, eliminating hunger. What possible reason justifies the continuation of hunger or starvation? None.

Respond to more needs. People in the world need to be fed. Respond to that need. Elderly people in nursing homes need to be visited. Respond to that need. Charities need volunteers. Respond to more needs. People in hospitals need to be visited. Respond to that need. Churches and charities need financial support. Respond to more needs. People who do their job well need to be acknowledged and appreciated. Respond to more needs.

Yeah, solving the world's problems is rather complex, difficult, overwhelming, inconvenient, costly and tiring. Respond to more problems anyway. Help one charity. Support one church. Visit one lonely senior citizen in one nursing home. Donate one can of food in a local food drive. Start a local food drive.

The quality of education in the United States concerns me. Although I am confident that schools do better work than they are given credit for, I know that improvements are needed. No one person can go to every school and teach every student. Each teacher can do the best possible teaching work with his or her students. Each teacher can respond to the needs of his or her students. Other people can support those admirable teachers.

When we each respond to the needs that we can do something about, the results will add up to problems solved, lives changed, hope fulfilled and differences made.

68. RESPOND TO OPPORTUNITIES

Sensitivity. Awareness. Response. Respond to opportunities is a version of respond to needs, but a person lives more vibrantly by responding to needs and by responding to opportunities.

Sensitivity. Awareness. Response. In this use of sensitivity the word conveys alert senses especially the mental, cognitive, intellectual ones. Be alert, be informed, be inquisitive. Know that there is always more to be known, to explore, to learn, to accept, to reject. That is right, to reject. Wise living means being highly selective.

Now that you are alert and informed, inquisitive and knowledgeable in general as a way of thinking and of looking at life, be aware of what can be done that advances you toward your intended results. If you have become informed that a new apartment building will be announced soon, but there is no benefit to you in considering living there, pay no attention to the announcement of the new development. Chasing every possible opportunity would result in a life of continuous chasing. Selectively pursuing the most advantageous opportunities which support your intended results is much more practical and productive.

Response. Now that we have moved through the steps of sensitivity and awareness, it is time to respond. No is a very effective response in many circumstances. For the college student who has a test tomorrow, no is the only prudent reply to a 10:00 p.m. question of, "Do you want to go to the party? It's starting right now."

A friend in another city offers you a job. He knows you are not looking for a new job, but he is looking for highly-skilled people and you have all the necessary skills. You, your spouse, your children are very settled in and pleased with the community where you live. You politely reject the offer. Five years later your friend's company is very successful or maybe five years later your friend has to close his business. You made the proper decision at the time based on everything you were devoted to, everything you valued and everything you intended to accomplish.

College students have many opportunities to be involved in campus activities. Beware. Many of those activities are beneficial while others are everything from a waste of time to a destroyer of reputations. Select the opportunities which serve the most important, the most honorable purposes.

Respond to opportunities. The response might be yes or no, but it should be certain and definite. Maybe is not a response. Opportunities cannot respond to maybe. Saying no to one opportunity enables you to say yes to another. The opportunity you said no to probably will not return. Saying yes to the opportunity means saying no to others–for yes to work it requires 100 percent yes. Maybe is vague, unsure. With maybe you are faced with a fork in the road and you just stand there and look, but never move.

Thinking comes before deciding and then acting. Action without prior thinking is a process of failure that could have been avoided. Thinking without subsequent action is a process of contemplating life instead of fully living life. Respond to opportunities.

List some opportunities you have responded to, what your response was and what the impact of that response was. Think, also, of what would have happened with a different response. What does this reflection reveal?

Opportunities	Response	Impact of That Response

Impact of a Different Response:

Overall insights from this reflection:

69. BELIEVE MORE DEEPLY

What do you believe in? How deep are those beliefs? Have those beliefs been examined and did they pass the challenge of questions, doubts, frustrations, disappointments and despair? Did those beliefs thrive only in time of joy, great achievement, victory and reward?

What do you believe in? Why do you have those beliefs? Are your beliefs based on how your family has believed, how your community believes, how your friends believe, how your colleagues believe, or maybe just, well, you've always believed the way you do and never gave it much thought.

The flag of the United States. The U.S. Constitution. Family. God. The importance of education. Saving money. Keeping proper promises. Hard work. A healthy lifestyle. Daily exercise. Church. Prayer. Being honest. Playing fair. Telling the truth. Jesus Christ. Those beliefs and others are common. The question becomes how deeply do you believe?

If you believe in education, do you believe in it enough to read important books while your children do their homework so they see you studying also?

If you believe in honesty, do you tell the store clerk when you are given too much change?

If you believe in a healthy lifestyle, do you exercise daily and do you eat the proper food while avoiding unhealthy food?

If you believe that young people should not use vulgar language, do you set the example of clean language only?

If you believe that you should move to a new house, are you seriously investigating the local real estate market, or are you just hoping that something will happen?

If you believe enough to put the beliefs into action, then there is a depth to your belief which demanded action. A person who believes that being healthy is important, but eats a lot of junk food and never exercises has very shallow, superficial beliefs. Maybe, instead of believing in the importance of being healthy, that person is merely very slightly informed about good health, but is not a true believer who, by definition of true belief, puts the belief into action. Maybe that person is in a fantasy.

Action may provide the most accurate insight about beliefs. Reflect on your actions. What do you spend more time on each day? Perhaps the highest quantity of time reflects the deepest level of belief. Ok, we sleep one-third of our life, but we do not have strong convictions about sleep other than to realize that enough is good, too little or too much would be bad.

During the hours that you are awake, what activity gets more time from you than all others? What activity gets your total effort? No matter the amount of time involved, what activity gets the totality of your effort or the majority of your effort?

How much time we put into our effort and how much effort we put in our time can reveal the depth of our beliefs. List your beliefs. List your commitment of time each day to everything you do so the total is 24 hours. Then list, from 100 percent to one percent, how fully you dedicate yourself, ranging from a total effort with each activity you do daily to little or no effort. What do the results tell you? Are you satisfied with the results?

Believe. Believe more. Believe more deeply.

70. HOPE MORE

Eleven at night on a Friday in late July 2007 and the emergency room at the hospital was unusually quiet with one exception. An expert team of six medical care professionals were preparing my mother for immediate surgery. Mother had fallen about 45 minutes earlier and severely broken her right ankle in two places. One piece of fractured bone had severed the skin causing a 6-inch laceration and much loss of blood. My arrival brought some hope and encouragement to my mother. An emergency room is a place where there is an unlimited need for hope and a limited supply of hope.

By 4:45 a.m. on Saturday mother was out of surgery and was ready to move from the post-operation setting to her hospital room. She needed to sleep, so she went to sleep and I went home.

Saturday afternoon mother rested well, was alert and conversational, had a good appetite and through her actions assured her family that she would recover. She was surrounded by family which meant the room was full of faith, hope and love.

Bless her heart, mind, body and soul, mother had endured more than her share of life's pain, agony and difficulty during her then 80 years. She is legally blind due to macular degeneration which gradually, but relentlessly, stole increasing parts of her vision for the past 35 years. There is no cure. The best treatments seem to be lasers, faith, hope and love. She has had many blessings and joys in life, but in time of severe sadness it is difficult to see beyond the current pains and its reminder of past pains.

About 7:00 p.m. on Saturday, mother asked a very realistic question: "Am I dying?" God had decided already that this was not to be the time of mother's death; however, a series of serious complications had suddenly emerged to make her question realistic. She was surrounded by five relatives, all of whom sincerely prayed and desperately hoped.

The hospital's rapid response team was pure perfection as they applied crisis management skills to bring stability and improvement to mother's condition. That team has medical knowledge which they apply expertly. To me they were sources of hope, they were reasons to hope.

During Sunday and Monday my thoughts changed completely. I had asked myself repeatedly what I could have done to prevent this injury which my mother had experienced. Looking backwards gave me ideas that never could have actually occurred when time was moving forward. Those lessons learned will be applied in the years that I hope I can be of unprecedented help to my mother.

My thoughts changed from what I could have done to what I can do now, tomorrow, throughout mother's life to be more helpful.

Those thoughts emerged from a conclusion that God almighty had decided that mother had more life to live. I hope that I can help make the rest of her life as joyous as possible. If God has decided that mother is to live, I will not debate what God or I could have done to prevent mother's injury; rather, I will pray, hope and work to support her recovery and her life after she is well.

My hope has a picture which displays what success will look like, which illustrates hope fulfilled, which would be a miraculous answer to many prayers. Here's that scene.

On an otherwise typical Sunday in October, my hope envisions, mother will be well and I will take my mother to the church where she has been a faithful member for over 60 years. Her presence there can confirm to anyone who sees her worship, the presence of God, the love of God, the healing power of God, the promises of Jesus Christ in ways which touch the lives of everyone at church that day.

My hope manifested includes mother being with her family at Thanksgiving and at Christmas. Tomorrow is promised to no person. Tomorrow can be and is hoped for.

Hope is not magic or fantasy. Hope is not illusion or deception. Hope is the start of a sequence which, for our family, includes prayer and actions, more prayer and more action. The prayers and the actions may bring about exactly what was hoped for, less than that or more than that. Life is lived better with hope and with the sequence of faith-inspired work which hope ignites.

This is a time to hope as I have never hoped before, a time to believe, love and work as never before. I hope therefore I act, taking more and better action than I would have thought possible at all, certainly more and better action than I would have thought possible from me.

Dear God, please completely and quickly heal my mother and, in doing that, give new hope to people who thought that some situations in life are hopeless.

Author's note: My mother did get back to church on Christmas Eve, five months after the July injury. It was a time of much joy for many people who welcomed her and were thankful that hope had been fulfilled.

71. LOVE MORE

There are two possibilities: 1) love more people; 2) express a deeper, more active, complete love to people whom you already love.

Love more people. This does not mean that you should stroll along the sidewalk of Main Street in your hometown and approach every person with a greeting of "I love you." The response would be a concern for your people skills and your mental health.

Love more people does mean that, to start with, the interactions you have with other people in the regular activities of life will be done more lovingly. A person calls you and states, "The past few days have been so difficult. My father is in the hospital and the company where I work is cutting our hours. I don't know what to do." Your reply is not, "You think that's bad? I have to spend $1,000 to get my car fixed and my dentist told me that both of my children need braces. I can't afford all of that."

A more loving reply could be, "If you need your children to stay here with us when you go see your father at the hospital that is fine. Just let me know. I think my company is looking for some part-time help with very flexible hours. I'll get an application for you and I'll find out more. Maybe you can apply online. I can recommend a great orthodontist who works with you on finances. We've been friends for years. We'll get you through all of this."

Within the comprehensive word love are many components. Love includes kindness, thoughtfulness, compassion, being there, polite manners. The medical staff at the hospital will provide expert care for the patient, but family members provide an essential medicine for the heart, mind, body, and soul–being there. Sometimes love merely requires being there, so loving more can be as fundamental as being there more. More means more time and more attention to people during that time. Expressions of appreciation and praise to the hospital staff are not mandatory, but are ways to love more.

For people whom we already love, the opportunity to love with a depth, a perfect certainty, a completeness is what love more can mean. Love more does not suggest days of bliss and joy. "No, you will not have any ice cream because you did not complete the chores that you had to do this afternoon. There is plenty of food on your plate, so you will not be hungry. Tomorrow, do the chores and you may have ice cream." This action is direct, straight-forward, clear, realistic and is loving the child more than giving in to the child's complaining or irresponsibility because "well, she had a busy day and the chores really can wait, so just this once I'll go along."

Love more. A very busy married couple could set aside Thursday nights as the time of never staying at work late, never scheduling a meeting to attend, never letting anything that can be controlled get in the way of being together on Thursday nights. Of course, the couple would be together every night, but errands to run, volunteer work to do, an offer from friends to attend an event could arise. "No, Thursday is our time together. We are at home, we are together, we talk, we listen, we sometimes play a game, we listen to music, we concentrate on being together. It's our date night. It's just one way to love each other more, better, deeper."

Love more is an option available to everyone. I was getting on the elevator at a retirement residential building and I said to the elderly lady who was also entering the elevator, "Good morning. How are you?" Her reply was unique and honest, "Homesick. I'd rather be in Michigan. For some reason I agreed to move here."

We talked about how beautiful summer in Michigan can be. She spoke of her home there as a promised land. We agreed that summer in Kentucky could be pleasant also. I encouraged her to make the most of the day. My comments did not change her preference for Michigan, but I hope that it was helpful that her "homesick" reply was acknowledged, taken seriously and understood.

Love more. Love more people. Love more people with more love. As I write these words the question for myself is "What keeps me from loving more?" and I quickly realize that no answer is satisfactory. The only solution to realizing that I have not loved more is to actually love more. Some parts of living well are quite obvious.

Imagine the anguish, regret, burden, shame and sadness associated with the realization that we could have loved more, but that we just did not do that. "I could have called more often." "I could have visited more often." "I could have been there just to show

I care. Certainly they know I care, don't they?" Take the proper loving actions that create the certainty so they know.

Loving more means loving more right now. Love more now. What is more important than love and when is a better time than now? For details about what love is and what love is not, read the 13th chapter of 1 Corinthians in the Bible.

72. SEEK MORE WISDOM

The United States of America has properly paid tribute in many ways to the generation which sacrificially, respectfully, obediently, courageously, willingly and successfully fought World War II. In some ways it is possible that this nation peaked with that generation and with the most significant achievement of that generation.

How did the World War II generation become the quality people who defended this nation and our allies? There must have been much wisdom in the generation which reared the World War II soldiers and the World War II citizens who supported the war effort by sacrifice in war and by involvement at home.

My grandparents reared a few members of the World War II generation. Contemporaries of my grandparents reared millions of other members of the World War II generation. For those of us who are baby boomers born during 1946 to 1963, our parents fought World War II, yet our grandparents made our parents the people who were ready, willing, and able to win World War II. What did our grandparents know that enabled them to instill wisdom into their children?

Manners is the starting point. I knew my mother's parents very well. Keen and Eunice Johnson were born in 1896 and 1895 respectively. He was born in Kentucky and she was born in Missouri. Their early years were filled with hardship, struggle and sacrifice in ways which never threatened survival, but which did instill a wisdom about what matters most in life.

Parents were to be honored and obeyed. Adults were to be spoken to very politely. Courtship had strict rules. Work was much more important and much more valued than entertainment. Church was attended, always and you sat still and listened. School was not to be liked or disliked; rather school work was to be done without grumbling and without delay.

When a life is structured on proper manners some problems are avoided, some mistakes are prevented and what is now termed "people skills" becomes part of how you live. Manners help instill self-control, self-discipline, a foundation for a sense of ethics and a realization that right and wrong are clearly identified.

A dear couple, now in heaven, who were close friends of my grandparents and of my parents, were married with total devotion to one another for 70 years. They lived most of the 20th century and a few years of the 21st century. Dr. Adron Doran and his dear, beloved wife, Mrs. Mignon Doran, exemplified the wisdom, character, charm, work ethic, manners, discipline, decorum, grace and integrity of the generation which preceded the World War II generation.

Dr. Doran served as president of Morehead State University in Kentucky for 23 years. Mrs. Doran was a gracious, vibrant First Lady of the University. Thousands of students can attest that their lives were changed favorably by acts of kindness, encouragement, guidance, discipline and love given by the Dorans.

Dr. and Mrs. Doran were perfectly polite, mannerly people. My grandparents, Governor and Mrs. Johnson, were perfectly polite, mannerly people. The Doran and Johnson examples are filled with wisdom. That wisdom emerges from an approach to life that begins with manners. Manners begin with a definitive certainty that some behavior, some actions, some interactions, some words are good while other behaviors, actions, interactions, words are bad, awful, unacceptable, wrong. From that foundation emerges a basis for wisdom that applies to all parts of life.

One precious source of wisdom is from a generation that lived honorable, exemplary lives beginning a century or so ago. To reclaim their manners and their wisdom is to reclaim part of the best of America, of mankind, of life.

73. READ EVEN MORE GOOD BOOKS

Twenty-two books, 4,106 pages. Promise made and kept. My project list for the summer of 2007 was to read, read more and keep reading. The inspiration was that I had just completed a year of teaching high school United States history classes after having worked as a middle school assistant principal for the prior 13 years. With topics such as U.S. History, the more you learn the more you realize there is more that can be learned. I learn best by reading so June and July 2007 became a time of continuous independent study.

The result was not at all what I expected. The result was better. The 2007-2008 school year began well, but with each topic the students and I discussed, my thought was that I should know much more than I knew. I told the students that for every topic mentioned in every paragraph of a U.S. History textbook, expert historians had written a dissertation, a book or both. I decided to lead by example, to teach by example.

When the next topic would be Jacksonian Democracy, I would read a biography of Andrew Jackson a few days before the students and I began the discussion of President Jackson. They were always amazed at the details I could provide. Those details provoked questions, ideas, curiosities from the students. The result was more learning, better learning, plus an element of fascination which energized our work.

The next step was to occasionally read a paragraph from one of the books I read to the students. I would pass the book around the class for everyone to see. The young scholars were realizing that history is not what gets squeezed into 1,000 pages of a high school textbook. History is the totality of what has been experienced, endured, achieved, confronted, and learned so far in the human endeavor.

During the December 2007 Christmas vacation I read five books about the history of the United States. I know that an hour of reading might become only one minute of insights I can share with my students. The hour of reading was compelling to me. The one minute of enhanced learning will be beneficial for the students and will give me a valuable sense of superior accomplishment. I could teach without doing the extra reading. I teach better when I do extra reading. When better is possible, better is mandatory based on ethics, conscience and honor.

Read even more good books. What about reading information from websites? What about reading an article from a magazine or journal? What about reading an article from a newspaper? All of those can be worthwhile, beneficial and productive. Still, they are literary appetizers, or perhaps appeteasers is a better description.

A good book is a full course meal. Books are designed with a comprehensive concept in structure and in content. If you need a fact or two, an article will suffice. If you seek a depth of knowledge and of understanding, books are required reading.

Read even more books. When the hands hold, the eyes see (or with audio books, when the ears hear), the brain processes, and the mind analyzes, extraordinary learning can occur.

"But I'm all about the internet. The only reading I do is a website or a text message. My friends and I are laptop, cell phone and things like that only. Books are so slow. Books are so old. Books, you know, books are just not how we find out anything."

You can find out a lot through a laptop, cell phone or other electronic devices. Don't limit yourself to what can be found out. Expand to what can be learned, analyzed, explored, explained, known, and understood. Some ideas, some knowledge, some insight will come to you only through interaction with a book. The internet is known for providing information. Books are known for providing knowledge and understanding. Try e-books to get the book depth within the electronic process.

Read more good books. Read more good books, keep reading good books. As long as there are good books which you have not read, an improved life is only 250 pages and some hours of reading away. Investing those hours in productive, wholesome reading can provide benefits for a lifetime. Why turn down that offer?

Read more good books. Then read even more good books. Books are different from other writing in many ways, one of which is the presentation of book-length ideas. Whether a hard copy of a book or the electronic twin of that hard copy, reading good books is great mental exercise and is essential to gaining knowledge.

74. REMEMBER MORE BIRTHDAYS

When you teach high school juniors it becomes rapidly obvious that two days stand out in their junior year of high school. Those two days are their birthday and the day they get their driver's license. The smile on a high school junior's face that emerges when she or he can tell the world "I got my license" is a unique expression of pure joy.

Birthdays are important to high school students in ways which might surprise some people. Toddlers and children cherish their birthday celebration. The birthday party of a two-year-old, 8-year-old or 12-year-old can become a major holiday occasion. The birthday of a high school student has similar excitement even as the method of celebration changes. What seems to matter most is the act of noticing, of acknowledging the student's birthday.

A student whom I taught 20 years ago always gets a birthday card or letter from me annually. That student always calls me on my birthday. The letter versus the call may reflect differences in generations. He works in upper management for a telephone and communications company. I write books. We remember each other in a formal way annually. I remember that student throughout each school year whenever I am asked about what is required for a student to achieve magnificently. Listen, think, ask questions, answer questions, do more than is required, read, work, manage time well, behave. In his very successful career he uses the same skills. In his very successful career he also uses the same people skill that is evidenced each year by my phone ringing about 8:00 p.m. followed by a cheerful, "Happy birthday, Dr. B."

Remember more birthdays. To acknowledge another person's birthday is to do more than notice the person. It is to notice their membership in the human community. A sincerely expressed happy birthday also communicates a joy that the person was born and a further joy that your lives have intersected.

For 20 years I have given my nephews and my niece a birthday gift of one $2 bill for each year they are celebrating. On a

10th birthday, the gift was 10 $2 bills. They have each collected these $2 bills throughout the years and now have wonderful collections. They always know that their birthday will include that same gift which marks the occasion annually. There is no possibility of anyone getting weary of this annual repetition. It is part of what we do, what we expect, what we find value in and what we find shared joy from. So, in these cases, how the birthday is remembered adds a continuity of commitment.

Teaching high school seniors who reach age 18 brings another shared experience. As their social studies teacher I get to share with them their excitement about being old enough to vote and to affirm with them the importance of taking voting seriously. I also affirm with them the importance of their vote. The action of remembering more birthdays, including the 18th birthday and the voting responsibility it brings, is a way to personalize interest and shared experience.

Every person should hear "Happy Birthday" and read "Happy Birthday" on their birthday. Making sure that people in nursing homes, in hospitals, in orphanages, in schools, in offices, in churches, in remote corners of the globe hear and read "Happy Birthday" is one way to tilt the balance of life toward goodness. Think of the people in your neighborhood, in your city, in your sphere of influence for whom you could be the only person who says "Happy Birthday" and go be a messenger of God, an angel, a saint who keeps one person from thinking or from experiencing the silent anguish that nobody remembered their birthday.

75. LEARN FROM GRANDPARENTS

Life would be lived much better if I could be more like my grandparents. Why? Why should I be more like those people who were born in the 1890s? Simple. They knew how to live a life that really mattered because they had learned throughout their lives what really matters.

Tom Brokaw's masterpiece, *The Greatest Generation*, properly and eloquently honors the Americans who fought the necessary fights of World War II. What made the people in the World War II generation capable of rising to the challenge, task and duty which confronted them? You remember the answer - the generation which reared the greatest generation.

My brother and I were born in the 1950s, very typical baby boom offspring. Our parents were born in the 1920s, very much destined to be in the World War II generation that would then also win the post-war peaceful return to regular life. Our grandparents were born in the 1890s and they were the ethical, moral, faithful foundation upon which "The Greatest Generation" was built, reared, and educated.

There are numerous lessons that can be learned from my grandparents, including

1. Save money
2. Save more money
3. Keep saving money

They were born in a decade which had an economic depression, the 1890s. They were young adults with parental responsibilities during The Great Depression and they knew the urgency of pinching pennies.

I recall going to downtown Richmond, Kentucky with my grandfather often. He knew everyone. Everyone knew him. I was in awe. We walked past a music store and I asked if we could go in. We left a few minutes later and I had a $1 record he purchased for me, although he told me clearly he thought it was not worth $1. He was right. 45 years later the record and the $1 are gone. The lesson to not waste money endures.

Grandparents through the years are sources of wisdom who know the importance of the lasting, meaningful parts of life. Other lessons from the wisdom of grandparents include:

4. Obey your parents
5. Work hard
6. Play fair
7. Be friendly and polite
8. Say your prayers
9. Help other people
10. Get all the education possible
11. A good reputation can be damaged or destroyed in one bad moment
12. The most precious gift is time, make the most of it
13. People are more important than things
14. Live up to the commitments you make
15. Tell the truth
16. Find ways to do something good for other people and to say something kind to other people
17. Apologize when you are wrong or even close to wrong
18. Devote yourself to your family.

My grandparents were devoted to each other until death did they part. They had perfect manners. They were of the highest ethics. They were what I hope to be. They were the generation that made possible "The Greatest Generation." They were more than the greatest. They made the greatest possible.

76. HEAR MORE GREAT SYMPHONIES

Beethoven's 9th and Beethoven's 5th symphonies remind me of the possibility of perfection. To hear those symphonies is to encounter the ideal, the ultimate, the essence of music, the very best of music.

What makes a symphony a symphony? At first glance the list of essentials would include an orchestra complete with musicians, musical instruments and a conductor. That is not enough.

The written music itself is required. The composer had to identify each note which is to be played upon each instrument throughout the total duration of the symphony. That is not enough.

A concert hall is important. The proper acoustics in the concert hall will enhance the symphonic experience. Comfortable seating, clear lines of sight from each audience member to the stage will be beneficial. Some artistry within the architecture, design and appearance of the concert hall will be useful. Still, that is not enough.

There must be an idea. The sheet music is not a random collection of disjointed notes. The sheet music is the expression of an idea which might have been put into words by an author, into strokes by an artist, into movement by a dancer, into shapes by an architect, yet which have been put into notes by a composer. The unique notes of each instrument were chosen as the best way to express the composer's idea.

To listen to great symphonies is to stretch the mind beyond the possible toward the perfect. The orchestra and the conductor present their performance, their understanding, their experience of the music as one manifestation of the idea which the composer had in mind, in heart and in soul during the time of composition. Another orchestra with a different conductor will present a performance that differs in important, honorable, valid and intriguing ways. Such is the power of an idea to exist, to inspire, to transform, to appear and to reappear without limits.

Hear more great symphonies does not mean merely to tolerate the sounds of Beethoven in the background while chores are done at home or while miles are driven in a car. To hear more great symphonies means to fully concentrate on the symphony. To hear requires the total attention of an active mind which interacts with the music always asking, seeking, analyzing, listening, wondering, experiencing, being and becoming.

There are many other forms of music besides symphonies, so why emphasize symphonies? There was plenty to do in Europe so why did Columbus sail across the Atlantic? There was plenty to do on planet Earth so why did the human travel to the moon? There is much simplicity in being single so why do 99 percent of human beings put themselves in the magnificent complexity of marriage? There is much comfort in the tranquility of staying in bed so why get up to confront the reality of a new day?

Great symphonies transcend sound, place, time and self. Great symphonies seek the eternal and reflect the soul. Great symphonies can remind us of the possibility of perfection. Much music or what passes for music fades away. The best symphonies reverberate forever as now is embraced by symphonic eternity past and symphonic eternity future. Great symphonies endure because quality endures.

Hear more great symphonies and in doing so hear the song from the soul of life longing to uplift you, longing to stretch your idea of yourself into the possibility of perfection.

77. MEMORIZE MORE

Poems. Speeches. Quotes. Stories. Wisdom. Advice. Scripture.

Earlier generations memorized more. Perhaps necessity was one reason. Prior to copy machines, television, tape recorders, radio, movies or the internet and computers, there was more value placed on embedding in the brain what machines now can retrieve and replay. Prior to books or electronics it was perhaps more likely to memorize because the brain had to hold in mental storage what the printed page would later hold in paper storage or what eventually a machine would hold in electronic storage.

What's the 21st century reason to memorize more? Urgency is one reason. That which is memorized can be used instantly. From time to time I have had the duty to tell a clerk at a retail store, "I think you gave me too much change." In elementary school I was taught old-fashioned arithmetic. We were required to do the math calculations in our head. I know the amount of change I am due because I know the difference between the total costs of the products purchased and the amount of money I am giving the clerk.

The clerk probably was not taught old-fashioned pencil and paper arithmetic. The clerk does know how the cash register works and trusts it to calculate everything. Whatever the machine says is owed, the clerk removes from the drawer. The machine could have been given inaccurate input. The money taken from the drawer for change may not match the correct amount which is owed. "I think you gave me too much change" is followed by the clerk realizing the error and (a) accepting the refund from me with repeated expressions of appreciation or (b) accepting the refund from me with little or nothing said. Memorizing math and memorizing manners–such as "thank you" would apply to such situations.

Why are those retail reality checks times of joy for me? I've memorized my comment to the clerk. "I want to be fair. That's what the Bible tells us. Do unto others as you would have them do unto you." The replies from clerks or cashiers have ranged from "Amen" to "yeah" to "no problem" to silence. I'm not going to sell my integrity for $1 of undeserved change. I will preach a short sermon in such situations in hopes that even if math is not learned, ethics and a Sunday School lesson can be learned.

The best speakers are not guided by a script or a mechanical monitor; rather, the best speakers know their content at the depth of conviction and with the certainty of memory. A preacher whose references to Bible verses are from memory and from conviction will have greater impact than a preacher who lacks one or both of those factors to any degree.

A high school graduation speaker who reads a script loses an audience. If the same speaker can look the graduates in the eyes, speak from his or her heart to theirs, quote vital statements with the emphasis that comes from memorization not cue card reading, the impact grows.

Memorize more for another reason. Life puts everyone in situations where there is no opportunity for lengthy analysis of options, the moment arises and a decision must be made now. What memorized words of wisdom will your mind give you at such moments? Only those which you have committed to memory. Be prepared. Memorize more.

The last reason to memorize more is almost ancient in rationale. Memorization is great exercise for the brain. The Lord's Prayer. The Gettysburg Address. A poem. A series of quotes. The 10 commandments. The best paragraph of the finest book you ever read. Statements by philosophers. Gems from family members. Know such words by heart, by memory, by commitment to truth. Exercise the brain, illuminate the soul, prepare the mind. Memorize more words of wisdom, pure words of eternal truth.

Memorize more and share what you memorized with others who seek truth, who need truth or who just find, or could with your help find, ideas to be compelling.

78. LEARN MORE LANGUAGES

Bonjour. The French have a charming, optimistic, cordial way of greeting each other. Bonjour is more than hello; rather it expresses literally the thought "good day". To know how ideas and thoughts, greetings and expressions are communicated in various languages is to expand the mind, is to enhance experience and is to explore the wonder of the activity of words.

My teaching and school administration experience includes many years of working directly with a Spanish immersion program. The students who began in this program as kindergarten students were immersed in Spanish for an increasingly significant part of the school day. By grades six, seven, and eight they were taught by native Spanish speakers for half of each school day, including math and science classes, with no English spoken. During those middle school years the young scholars attained fluency as they spoke, heard and thought in Spanish. Something wondrous was happening in their brains as they learned a new language and as they learned math and science in that new language. Learning a new language gives the brain a workout which is unique and that keeping the brain in only one language cannot simulate.

In recent decades the assumption often was that the world would learn English so people who were native English speakers did not need to learn another language. Such thinking was short-sighted at best and arrogant at worst. Just as the U.S. dollar may not forever be the one and only dominant international currency of record, the English language may not forever be the dominant international communication method of choice. As parts of the world which speak languages other than English become more involved in and more impactful on the world economy, the languages of those nations may be as vital to know as is having access to the products from those nations which are commonly purchased.

The 21st century is going to be a global century in ways that the 20th century was not. The languages of the globe will not defer to English just as the economies of the world will not defer to the U.S.

economy. Economies will compete and will cooperate. Knowing the language of your competition removes your competitor's advantage of knowing your language, and could also enhance cooperation.

Languages express the culture, the personality, the history, the uniqueness of nations and regions. To know French, Spanish, Chinese, Arabic, Japanese, Russian or other world languages is to also know of the culture of places where those languages are spoken.

I took seven semesters of French in college. The vocabulary is still etched in my memory; however, the appreciation of French culture, art, history, lifestyles, and priorities are also strong memories.

Learning other languages helps to exercise the brain, strengthen the mind, awaken new awareness and create new opportunities. In the 21st century the rest of the world is learning more languages. That example must be followed and surpassed or the world, with its languages and all they communicate, will leave the United States wondering what went wrong and why the American Century of 1901-2000 was not followed by an entitled sequel. The 21st century gives every indication that entitlements in the world community are being replaced by earned results. Learning other languages is one requirement of fully experiencing the global economy, the global village, the global wonders of now and of the future.

79. HELP MORE CHARITIES

A letter from a charity arrives. Yes, they are asking for money. Yes, the cause is worthy and the money goes to the cause. Yes, the people who are served by the charity need help which the charity expertly, efficiently, and lovingly provides. Writing a check for the charity is helpful and is important. Responding to every charitable request with a financial contribution is not possible. There are other donations.

Time. A person who donates four hours per month to answer the phone for her church is saving the church the money it would cost to pay a person to answer the phone. There's more. The church member who is volunteering to answer the phone is interacting at the church and on the phone with current church members, with prospective church members, with local community members, with people who need help, with people who are offering help, with the range of questions that fill every day at a church.

This same volunteer now has a different awareness of, appreciation of, understanding of, and opportunity to support the church. The answer is almost always the same–who benefits more, the person who volunteers or the organization the volunteer helps? Right, the person does. It's almost as if volunteering is a perfect bonus of selflessness as you give of yourself yet you are giving to yourself simultaneously.

What is in the attic, the basement, the bedroom closet, or the garage that you have no use for, yet which could be a treasure for someone else? Clothes, a bicycle, books, furniture, or luggage are examples of what fills your home to an uncomfortable capacity yet, if donated to a charity, could fill another person's life with unlimited joy. Sometimes, life is really simple to improve, to impact favorably, to embrace.

Tell other people. Select that one charity in which you fully believe. Work with that charity so a letter you write is sent to the hundreds of people whom you know–friends, neighbors, your colleagues, people you do business with, people you know from church, people you went to school with. Your letter tells those people about the charity, what the charity means to you, and what their support of the charity would mean to you and to people who will be helped. Your letter includes information about several ways people could help the charity–donation of clothes, volunteer work, money–and includes a reply card or envelope. It is possible that some people will support a charity because that charity matters to you and you matter to those people.

Help more charities. To every problem there is an equal and opposite solution. The solution to the problems that most concern you could be to provide additional help to the charities which exist to help solve those problems.

80. VISIT MORE PARKS

Nothing fancy. No roller coasters or other automated rides. No massive screen theaters. No expensive souvenirs, concessions or parking. No cartoon characters roaming around. Certainly, such places can be entertaining, but amusement parks emphasize amusement more than they do park and they can be very expensive. In my hometown there are many, many parks which are often driven by, but far less often are they visited, experienced, explored. The people who do spend time at the parks are more in touch with the purity of and the beauty of this community's natural appeal than those of us who drive past the part of nature which is on display at parks.

Woodland Park is one of the natural gems in the Lexington, Kentucky community. Over 150 years ago some of the land which is this park was part of Henry Clay's estate. Mr. Clay was wise to appreciate the land. He would be surprised with the additions of a swimming pool, tennis courts, skate board facility and basketball courts. He would be pleased that the park is defined by an abundance of trees which create several natural domes as decades of growth have made these many trees among the most distinctive features of any park in the community.

For Woodland Park no official reservation is needed. The community has reserved this land for everyone to share, to experience, to encounter, to know. The challenge is to reserve your time to go to the park so the park does not become an "oh yeah, that is a good place to visit" missed opportunity as you drive past it in a blur as what cannot wait overtakes what might have been.

Years ago a friend suggested that we play tennis on a hot July Saturday afternoon. Great idea! She then suggested, "How about Woodland Park?" I paused thinking we could do better, certainly we could find a more exclusive, isolated place. I decided to defer to her suggestion. She was right.

Tennis courts surrounded by trees made tennis much more pleasant than tennis courts surrounded by concrete could ever be.

The best was yet to come. We walked through the park, found a park bench in a shaded area, sat and talked. Almost two hours later the discussion was still vibrant, the trees were still cordial, the park was continuously active, people came and went, other people replaced them. Everything just seemed to be so tranquil. One hopes that the park will be preserved forever.

Visit more parks. Visit means to stop, interact with, share time together, strengthen mutual appreciation, and when it is time to leave make a promise to visit again soon. Visiting the park is not a business meeting or an item to mark off from the day's to-do list. Visiting the park is reminding yourself that slowing down in a busy world can be very good.

81. WIPE AWAY TEARS AND HELP OTHERS DO THAT

Compassion means to suffer with. That's all, but that is a lot. Be there to suffer with people who suffer. Compassion does not require that you speak the perfectly eloquent words of comfort. Being there to suffer with people transcends the most eloquent statement. Being there is the strongest of all statements.

A person who is distraught, who is crying, who is weeping may not really hear any spoken words, but can find some strength in the presence of people who are there to mutually endure the tears, the heartbreak, the tragedy, the anguish, the sadness, the moments when life most hurts.

Does a person who is crying need someone else to actually wipe away their tears? Probably not, but it is a kindness initiative that could be appreciated. Perhaps you offer that crying person a tissue and that expression of concern itself is helpful. There is more to wiping away tears than the physical act of wiping away tears. Life hurts. Yes, in life there is, or can be, joy, there is hope, there is love, there is beauty, there is kindness, there is achievement, there are miracles and there are dreams that come true or, at least, can be pursued.

Still, life hurts. There are accidents that have forever impact. There is a sudden death that tragically cuts short a vibrant life causing the anguish of the moment followed by years of tears over what might have been. There is a factory closing that eliminates 1,000 jobs and 1,000 foundations for family stability. There is the car wreck that causes permanent disability and another car wreck that causes death. There is a medical condition that resists all treatment. There is an act of deception which destroys a friendship, a relationship, a family.

Life hurts. The hurts of life are accompanied by the tears of life. Yet, life goes on. The hurts do not destroy life; rather, they injure life for a time, they darken life for a season and they impact life perhaps permanently. We cannot reverse every hurt. We cannot uncry our tears. We can endure, cope, persevere. We can wipe away our tears and look anew at what life still offers while asking anew what we can offer to life.

Wipe away tears. In dealing with the sadness, the pain, the agony, the tragedy that life includes, the tears must be shed and must be wiped away. Then what?

Compassion must extend beyond the suffering season. To suffer with someone, to be there when the tears flow, to wipe away more tears, must be followed by encouragement therapy. When people attend a visitation or a funeral to offer kindness, compassion, hugs, stories, memories, and tributes, the family members of the deceased will benefit from those thoughtful expressions. After the funeral, after the burial, then what? Has the sadness stopped merely because the casket is in the ground? No, which means that compassion and encouragement are still needed.

Suffering will continue as long as life continues. Tears will flow and will need to be wiped away as long as human beings live. Sadness cannot be prevented, but sadness can be treated. Wipe away your tears and embrace what goodness in life you can find or you can create. With enough compassion from people who help others wipe away tears, suffering can be limited to punctuating life instead of defining or dominating life.

Wipe away the tears of other people and remind them of their ability to find goodness in life or to create goodness in life. Sadness, tragedy, anguish and tears do not define life; rather, they punctuate life. They are the pauses in, not the essence of, life.

82. READ TO CHILDREN

My grandfather, Keen Johnson, was born in 1896 and died in 1970. My memories of him are quite lively and vibrant, inspiring and impactful. My grandfather read to me when I was a child. I can still see and hear those precious hours of reading together. Reading to a child creates an immediate benefit and can create joyous memories that live for decades beyond the time of the reading.

When an adult takes the time to read to a child, there is more happening than reading. The brain of a child needs to be exercised and organized. When a child is read to the brain is exercised and that exercise enhances intellectual organization.

"I matter enough to you that you are taking time to read a story to me that you have read before, that you may not be very interested in hearing again and that I will ask you to read to me again tomorrow. When you do read it to me tomorrow, I will be as enchanted as if the story had never been read by anyone or heard by anyone. When you read to me, when you take your time to add to my life, I am shown what love looks like." A child's version of those thoughts would use simpler words, but would be just as strong.

Reading is love. Is that a stretch? Is that asking reading to do more or to be more than reading is capable of? "Ok, I've got 10 minutes. Get that book you've been pestering me to read to you." "Hey, Julie, it's book time. Let's go to the reading chair and get wrapped around your favorite book." Notice the difference in reading as chore and reading as love. Reading is occurring in both situations. The differences are in the atmosphere, the spirit, the tone, the how it was done versus what was done.

A close partner of reading to children is reading so children see you reading. As the child learns to read, the child joins in family reading time which is vastly superior to television, video games, social media or family isolation with everyone secluded in separate rooms. Tuesday night, for an hour, everyone in the family is in the family room reading. I have reason to believe that my grandfather and his parents shared hours like that. They have set a wise example to follow.

Read to elderly people and to blind people. The opposite of a child who is eager to learn to read might be an elderly person or a visually impaired person for whom reading is no longer possible. For these people, reading was once an important part of life, but now is pure frustration or not possible at all.

Books on tape or disc are helpful. Books via radio or local access cable television are helpful. Books read by one person to another person surpass what any tape or broadcast can accomplish. It is another example of reading as love.

Who am I? What can I do? There are so many problems in the world. If you are literate and if you will share part of your time, you can touch the life of a child, an elderly person or a visually impaired person by reading to them. If you put your heart and soul into it you will be reading with them. At that point you can't tell where the reading stops and the love starts because they are simultaneous.

83. LIFE HURTS

Reality must be confronted again. There are times in each life when life hurts. There are times when overall life in general seems to be painful.

There is much in life that is purely wondrous, majestic, beautiful, inspiring, lovely and precious. Sunrise. Stars. A baby's smile. A devoted couple celebrating their 50th wedding anniversary with the unique joy of husband and wife who were meant to be together forever.

It is good, it is necessary, it is essential for there to be much in life that is magnificent because there is also so very much in life that is tragic, painful, criminal, abusive, cruel, hateful, heart-breaking, evil and inexplicable.

Life hurts. For anyone who reads a newspaper there are numerous articles which confirm that life hurts. It's as if the newspapers are not reporting news, but are reporting pain, tragedy, cruelty, sadness and agony. Life does not hurt all of the time for most people, but the possibility and the reality of life hurting are not to be denied.

Life hurts. Of course, everyone knows that death will occur. Our challenge is to live so mightily that we outsmart death by leaving behind lives we touched, differences we made, people we loved, charities we supported, churches we built, friends we encouraged, neighbors we helped, children we reared, students we taught.

Death hurts, especially when it is too soon. I have known people in their 80s or 90s who were at perfect peace with death. Life had been good to them and they had been good to life. They were ready to live in heaven. Other people were very ready to stay on Earth and their age indicated they had more years to live, yet death happened. Life can hurt.

The newspaper reports an infant's death, a child's death in an awful accident, a teenager's death in an automobile wreck, or recently married couple's death when a crime happened on their honeymoon, a family member's death while trying to rescue a loved one who fell into raging waters. Life hurts.

Disease. Injury. Divorce. Financial failure. War. Fires destroying homes. Crimes destroying lives. Evil destroying hope. Hate destroying love. Agony destroying faith. Life hurts.

Confront the hurt. Do not deny the hurt. Do not take a detour around the hurt. Life knows it hurts. Hurt is part of life. Confront it. Get advice on how to endure it. Learn something from it and then emerge with a realistic appreciation of what is good and a realistic way to confront what hurts.

Pray throughout the pain. Get advice throughout the pain. Get counseling throughout the pain. Do not deny the hurt, do not cover the hurt with false laughter, do not hide behind "It was meant to be" or "these things happen". Do admit the fact of the event that happened and the hurt it brought, do think and learn, do cry and hug, do endure, but not alone.

Life hurts. When life hurts, remember that it is vital, it is essential, it is helpful to draw strength, hope and encouragement from other people. The hurts of life are not intended to be tolerated and survived alone. Similarly, the joys of life are not intended to be hoarded or kept secret.

Life hurts. That is not the only description of life, the only reality in life or the only truth in life. Life hurts. That is a certainty which presents us with a question–what is our response to the hurts of life? We cannot prevent the hurts of life. We can control our response to the hurts of life. We are challenged to prevail amid the hurts, to respond courageously to the hurts and to emerge from the hurts with new strength and convictions.

Life hurts. Be prepared. Be strong. Acknowledge and express the pain. Surpass the hurt. Live vibrantly, bravely and with relentless determination.

84. SAVE MORE MONEY

"Save. Save More. Keep saving." In economics classes I have taught, those five words are instantly memorized by students very early on the first day of the class. Without fail, whenever I ask former students to tell me what they remember from economics class, their answer is "Save, save more, keep saving." Those words do stay in the brain. As one student explained, "You said it. I thought about it. And it is stamped on my brain for all eternity."

The challenge is to do what those words tell us is vital. The goal is not to be obsessed with money. The students are told, "Money is not the most important part of life. Family, other people, what you believe in, what you commit to and integrity are some parts of life that are more important than money. Still, if you manage the money part of life well, the other parts of life can be enhanced."

Save. Save more. Keep saving. The first step in saving is to make saving the top priority. No money is to be spent until some money has been saved. Money is spent when spending is necessary, not whenever spending is possible. Does that sound harsh? Think again. What happens when people spend, spend more, keep spending? Those people are probably in debt, are probably controlled by their debt, are possibly surrounded by the endless items they have needlessly bought through the years and are one unexpected expense away from financial disaster.

In the 1920s people started buying appliances and other products on the installment plan, rather than saving money and then paying in full. Is credit evil? It can be. Is saving evil? Never, so why take the risk?

Around 1949 or 1950 the first credit card appeared. Oops, beware. Sure, if a person pays the credit bill in full instantly when the bill arrives, there will be no finance charge; however, people tend to spend more when using a credit card than when using cash. You get to keep the credit card. You have to let go of cash when you use it. Cash helps keep us honest.

Save. Save more. Keep saving. How? Do not spend. Every optional purchase that you could make is money that you could save. "But I really have to buy that new dress." "But I really need to buy that new television." Is it life threatening to keep wearing the clothes you have? Is it life threatening to keep using the old television or to use television less and less?

Save. Save more. Keep saving. This does not mean to become a hermit, a recluse, a cave dweller, a horse and buggy advocate who is certain that cars are a temporary fad. Think. Think more. Keep thinking. Control your money so money does not control you. Save your money so the lack of money does not control you.

The United States national government is terribly irresponsible with its portion of the nation's wealth. For the U.S. national debt to have increased from $1 trillion in 1980 to over $16 trillion in 2012 is to have abandoned any concept of sensible financial management. While the national government has become addicted to debt, far too many U.S. citizens are becoming similarly addicted to debt. When the news reports a "negative saving rate", the translation is that people spent more money than they had and/or people reduced what savings they had built up. The errors of the 1920s which led to the Great Depression do not have to be repeated, but some of them are being repeated quite unnecessarily and quite unwisely.

Save. Save More. Keep saving. "But our economy is built on credit. People can't save up to buy a car or a house." An affordable, fixed rate, 30-year or 15-year mortgage on a reasonable home you will live in for a long time can make sense. For cars, finance your first car with payments of $300 per month. Pay it off in four years, keep it for 10 years. During years 5-10, pay your savings account $300 per month. At the end of year 10 you can pay cash for your next car and have the bargaining power cash provides. Then, save for the next 10 years and car buying will be very easy again. Why? Because you saved, saved more, and kept saving.

85. APOLOGIZE WHENEVER NEEDED

"I'm sorry."

"I was wrong. What can I do to make it up to you?"

"My fault. Completely my fault. I'm really sorry."

"I did not mean for that to happen. Let's fix it right now."

"My mistake. I'll do better next time."

"Please forgive me. Please tell me what I can do to make amends."

Imperfection is part of the human condition. Mistakes get made, some errors are intentional, some are unavoidable, some are preventable.

There are many, many times when people do exactly what they should do. You hire someone to clean your carpets and they do such outstanding work that you promise yourself to recommend them to other people. You teach a Sunday School class and every student arrives on time, is polite, listens, participates properly, and learns. Each family member has specific chores to do daily and those chores get done consistently.

Accidents occur. Mistakes are made. Irresponsibility, animosity, rudeness, vengeance, unkindness are all avoidable, but do happen. Life does not require perfection. Life lived well does require that we correct all that can be corrected.

"I lost your pen I borrowed. I'll bring you two pens just like that one tomorrow."

"I should have called you sooner. I knew I was going to be late. I'm sorry. We're too late for that movie, but we could still go out to supper and see the movie later if you'd like to. Whatever you prefer." A note, flowers, something else extra the next day is advised.

"I'm sorry. I know you told me to never use that kind of language. I was wrong. I know what the punishment is so I'll clean up everything after supper tonight."

Apologizing sincerely is one part of correcting a mistake. Taking action to make amends is another part. Taking extra care, caution and effort to prevent making the same mistake shows a good faith effort that confirms the sincerity of the apology.

Saying "I'm sorry" also serves the purpose of making the person who is apologizing confront the mistake, the cause of the mistake, the responsibility for the mistake, and the lessons which can be learned from the "mistake, apology, make amends" process.

American morality, manners, ethics and civility have declined in recent decades. Society does not advance when free speech becomes a 24 hour per day barrage of vulgarity and immorality from television, radio, movies, music, the internet, social media and more. Such media crudeness need not define who we are or who we become. As I have told high school students in recent years: "Adults owe you an apology, my generation owes you an apology. We have allowed television, music and movies to become such trash that you may think every sentence needs a few vulgar words in it. I'm sorry that has happened. For my part, you will never hear such language from me and I will never tolerate such language from you."

"I'm sorry."

"I was wrong. Let's work it out."

"It was my fault. I'll fix it and I won't let it happen again."

Those words can be powerful in healing human relationships that have experienced some damage. Those words spoken sincerely and followed with helpful action can do much good.

A student who had misbehaved several times in a week needed to be corrected more emphatically than I had done. We spoke in the hallway. He said, "I'm sorry." I replied, "No, you're not. I've heard that from you before. If you had been sorry this problem would not have continued." He was speechless. He was learning a lesson. "I'm sorry" has to be much more than words. It has to be implemented with helpful corrective actions. He had said "I'm sorry" before and obviously those words meant nothing because the misbehavior continued. An authentic, sincere "I'm sorry" must be matched with correction and proper behavior.

86. WHAT REALLY MATTERS

The New Testament of The Christian Bible tells of Jesus Christ encountering a crippled man who had been unable to walk for decades. Jesus has much compassion for the man and tells him to "pick up your mat, rise and walk." The joyous man does exactly as he was told, but there is some criticism of what should have been celebrated as a joyful, miraculous healing.

The healing occurred on a day when, according to rules and laws of that time and place, people were not allowed to carry their mats. "It is the Sabbath, the law forbids you to carry your mat." (John: Chapter 5)

To the mind of the law enforcer, carrying the mat was so offensive that the healing which made it possible for the formerly crippled man to rise, walk and carry the mat was not noticed or was not as important. How is that thinking possible?

How easy it is in life to miss, to overlook, to forget what really matters. In the pursuit of precision about the trivial we can miss the miraculous of the vital.

What really matters? There are no surprise answers. Touching lives really matters because each moment of each life really matters.

Amid all the day to day evil and agony, tragedy and pain, sadness and despair in life, there are moments when with some effort we can do what really matters. We can touch a life. That is part of what really matters and that helps us to really matter.

There are decisions, priorities and judgment calls. The child would really enjoy some ice cream and you would like to provide that enjoyment, but she barely touched supper and vegetables come before ice cream. What matters most at that moment is the long term lesson about nutrition and the parent exercising proper authority, not appeasing the yearning for ice cream.

When faced with rejoicing over the healing of a person who previously could not walk and micro-management of the most minute, legalistic, pointless rule about when a mat could be carried, the life giving choice is clear–rejoice and give thanks that the person can walk and carry the mat. Life is enhanced when we emphasize what matters most.

Think about the parts of life which matter most to you. Then think about the parts of life that should matter most to you. Are the lists identical? Are there some differences? What ideas can these lists provide?

What matters most to me now
-
-
-
-
-

What should matter most to me
-
-
-
-
-

87. BE MORE POLITE

"OK," "yeah" and "uh huh" never should have replaced "Yes, sir" and Yes, ma'am."

"No problem" never should have replaced "You're welcome."

Silence never should have replaced "Thank you".

Road rage never should have replaced sensible, calm, controlled driving with both hands on the steering wheel and no telephone in use. A phone conversation is less important than road safety.

Shouts, yells, whistling, air horns, cheers and other chaotic chanting from audiences at high school graduations never should have replaced respectful, self-controlled, silent unspoken yet deeply felt appreciation for the achievements of all graduates. Riotous ranting by one family is not as important as other families being able to hear and enjoy the program.

The adult who yells at the umpire, coach or player during a little league baseball game is inexcusably polluting the atmosphere and the experience.

The golf fan who has to yell "you're the man" or "in the hole" should stay at home so the other spectators can watch golf without barbaric noises disrupting an otherwise tranquil and pleasing experience.

Political candidates are convinced apparently that brutal rudeness is the only option for campaigning or for discourse. Such rudeness may hide a lack of ideas because if something sensible could be thought of, well, apparently nothing sensible can be thought of so slash and burn sound bites are used instead.

The incessant ringing of cell phones during church services, concerts, theatrical performances, funerals, classes at schools, weddings, and meetings is a symbol of selfish rudeness that is not justified by an inability to control one of technology's newest devices. This new technology gives more people more opportunities to be more impolite. Self-control and manners are still available to anyone who will make the effort. Technology and manners can co-exist.

What explains the decline of manners? What explains the rise of being impolite and the decline of being polite? One possible explanation is the increase of media filth including the sewage that is broadcast on television. From the most rude to the most bizarre, from the most vulgar to the most violent, a communication medium which impacts the viewers' purchase decisions via commercials also impacts the viewers other behaviors via program content. Movies and the internet share similar guilt.

Another possible explanation is popular music, well, popular notes and lyrics. It is an extreme stretch to describe some popular singing sounds or words as music. The content of some popular music today is a preview of and could be some evidence of a declining civilization.

Perhaps psychology distortions are another reason. For the cause of protecting self-esteem, a child whose action is rude, vulgar, immoral or illegal is told "you made bad choices" instead of "you were wrong." The implication is that the choice making mechanism malfunctioned instead of conscience, honor, integrity, and self-control were not applied.

Manners will improve when individuals rise above rudeness. Each "thank you", "you are welcome", "I'm sorry" or "please, you go ahead" are individual actions that create moments of manners. To every problem there is an equal and opposite solution. The problem of rudeness is solved by more people being polite.

88. CATCH MORE SNOWFLAKES

I hate snow. Snow has to be shoveled. Snow cancels events. Snow complicates traffic. I hate snow because it gets in the way. Still, I can dislike the snow or I can catch a snowflake with the wonder of a child or with the wonder of the child I once was. Perhaps we should not let the adult part of life so completely unchild us or unwonder us.

Some wonderful people graduated from high school yesterday. I was one of the teachers who volunteered to help with graduation. The gentlemen graduates were required to wear ties which, for some of them, was a new or nearly new experience. Some ties were available and my job was to get a tie on any male student who needed that help. It was an honor to offer that small gesture of help and encouragement.

"Are you an expert with ties?" I asked each student whom I helped. "No, sir. I think I've worn a tie once." We talked about their plans for life after high school. We smiled. The tie was tied, straightened and a sincere handshake completed the encounter. What might have been an awkward, nervous, frustrating minute for the 18-year-old almost graduate became a friendly visit. We caught a snowflake.

I watched the students throughout the graduation ceremony. Some tears were vastly outnumbered by endless smiles and hugs. Everyone was getting a diploma. Everyone was being congratulated. Everyone looked quite distinguished. Everyone caught a snowflake.

Throughout the one hour of final preparations before graduation, during the ceremony itself and then throughout the extended time of celebration, smiles and hugs, I cherished most the one-to-one conversations with students. The uniqueness of each student is confirmation that the human being is not a random intersection of energy, matter and time.

Each human being is created and throughout the life of each person that creation can be enhanced. Such was the work done to bring these young scholars to the moment of high school graduation.

The students I smiled with, talked to, congratulated, shook hands with had not randomly evolved for 18 years. They were reared by families, taught by teachers and guided by friends, mentors, coaches, neighbors, experiences and thoughts.

To give those students meaningful experiences which extend their capabilities, which challenge their skills, which encourage their achievements, which correct their mistakes, which reward their successes, which build upon their improvements, that is to catch more snowflakes, to see the beauty in the individual, to appreciate the wonder of being together.

What opportunities do we have, can we find, could we create to catch more snowflakes today? Please list some opportunities:

-

-

-

-

-

89. OVERCOME MORE OBSTACLES

Few, if any, lives are free of difficulties. The most privileged people who seem to have lives of luxury can encounter a tragedy, self-imposed turmoil, or a personal loss with deep pain.

Part of the definition of life, part of the truth of life, part of the inherent reality of life is that obstacles exist. How we encounter obstacles will determine who prevails–the obstacles or us.

Two soldiers return from war, both are very seriously injured. One overcomes the injury more than the other although the medical reality is that recovery was possible for both. Among the factors in one soldier recovering better than the other can be how they confront the obstacle of injury. Consider the following reactions to obstacles:

"I'll never lose those 20 pounds."

"I'll never get that credit card debt paid."

"My job is awful. Nobody should have to endure such conditions."

"I know what I promised. Some things came up. It's going to be very difficult to keep the promise."

"My grade is an F. How can I improve it? It's very late. Final exams are next week, so what can I do?"

How will the obstacle of the credit card debt be overcome? Can that be done? Stop using the credit card. Pay with cash when you buy something. Cut up the credit card. Negotiate a settlement and payment schedule with the credit card company. Get a second job. Have a garage sale. Doing nothing will not conquer this obstacle. Doing just anything is not rational. Analyze the obstacle, get wise advice, create a good plan to solve the problem, fully implement the plan.

Prevent obstacles whenever possible. Confront obstacles whenever necessary. Life comes with more obstacles than we expect. Life also comes with instructions in the form of wisdom from history and from advice of friends and family. Life comes with the option of confronting the obstacles or being overwhelmed by the obstacles. Your approach to and response to obstacles will be part of who you are and of who you become.

Think of obstacles which you face now. What are you doing to overcome them properly? What else could be done to completely overcome them in a proper way?

Obstacle	Actions Being Taken	Actions That Could Be Taken
•	•	•
•	•	•
•	•	•
•	•	•
•	•	•

90. STOP AT STOP SIGNS

Traffic is safer when everyone obeys laws of driving such as actually stopping at a stop sign or a stop light.

There are other stop signs in life, such as these:

- Stop eating so much junk food.
- Stop avoiding exercise.
- Stop the bad habit that is so harmful.
- Stop spending more money than you earn.
- Stop skipping breakfast.
- Stop watching so much television.
- Stop complaining about politicians, but never voting yourself.
- Stop phoning in sick when you are well.
- Stop ignoring family members who need your time, help, and attention.
- Stop playing the video game and go take the dog for a walk or take yourself outside for a walk if there is no dog.
- Stop regretting mistakes and missed opportunities; start taking action.
- Stop wishing that hungry people had food, start donating to food pantries.

Your turn. Add more stops which are important and meaningful to you.

- Stop

- Stop

- Stop

- Stop

- Stop

Now back to stop signs and stop lights. Children are told that red means stop. Children who observe many drivers would think that the meaning of red has changed.

Not stopping at a stop sign is arrogant, selfish, unwise, unsafe, and unhealthy. The five seconds it will take to fully stop, check both directions, and then continue could save a life or prevent a wreck. What's the value of five seconds saved when it results in a life lost?

Some people are faced with health problems that force them to stop habitual behaviors. It is healthy to not smoke tobacco products. The unhealthy impact of smoking tobacco can result in a person being forced to stop due to breathing difficulty, lung problems, or cancer. The brain or the lungs said stop smoking long before the physician demanded stop.

Let's practice. Stop reading this book right now. Go walk the dog. Go call a friend who needs help. Go hug your spouse. Stop denying, delaying and start doing. You can finish this book later. Touching a life needs to happen now for your good and for the benefit given to the other person.

91. SET BETTER EXAMPLES

He was the teacher who seemed to be at school all the time. If you arrived early, he was there. If you stayed for an after school activity, he was still there in his math classroom. He might be working with students who found algebra to be confusing. He might be grading papers. Years later his example still reminds me of what a teacher can be, can achieve, can do with and for students.

She was the friend who always mailed people a newspaper article that included their name or picture. Long before e-mail made such communications easy, she would read the newspaper, see an article about you, mail you the copy and never expect any acknowledgment. Her example of thoughtfulness reminds me to attach newspaper articles of interest to my students when I return a test. A student who plays lacrosse was very pleased with a New York Times article on college lacrosse that I gave him as I followed an example of kindness from years ago.

Every Monday morning I was asked how my weekend had been. The answer was usually, "A lot of school work. Many papers to grade." The caring student in my first period class would encourage me to not work too hard. That 17-year-old was setting a good example of greeting people on Monday morning.

She shows up. When a friend has a difficulty, she goes to that friend. She knows the healing power of being there. Her example of reaching out is genuine.

He calls or e-mails everyone who needs to know what he just found out. He knows how much those people value current information and updates. His example of pre-emptive communication is one of much impact and efficiency.

He always does much more than is required. On every project in our U.S. History classes, his projects were masterpieces. He expected that level of achievement from himself. His example of a high personal standard is inspirational.

Set better examples. Doing what is right is beneficial for the ethical person it helps you be and become, plus for the impact it has on people who notice your actions and then imitate you.

One career option I had right after college was given minimal consideration. I would have been very good at the work. I had the aptitude and the ability. I was accepted into the required education program. That option was not taken because I knew few young members of that profession who seemed to really like their work. Someone in that profession could have set a better example for me to consider. It could have been a great career.

In the moment-to-moment living of families, in the moment-to-moment work shared by colleagues, in the day-to-day tasks which everyone faces, how we do our work, how we treat each other, how we endure difficulties, how we celebrate successes, are all opportunities to set a great example. I will forever set the example for my students that speaking without vulgarity is both possible and preferred. Whether I know they are watching and listening or whether I am unaware of that, my example can impact them beyond what I realize. We are obligated to do what is right because it is right. Other people will benefit from seeing rightness in activity or by the presence of right action.

Set good examples. Touch the lives of those who see your good example and touch the lives of those who will apply your example now and long after your death. The powerful impact of a good example multiplies.

92. ACCEPT MORE RESPONSIBILITY

"It was my fault."

"I'll fix it."

"I can do that for you."

"Sure, I'll volunteer."

"I can help."

There are some vital and vibrant members of each community who seem to be involved in every major event, gathering, fundraiser, project, or celebration. These busy people are fairly likely to be the most willing people to accept more responsibility. It seems to be easier to get a busy person to take on more responsibilities than to get someone who is doing nothing to do something.

How did people who eagerly and repeatedly accept more responsibility begin living that way? Perhaps they saw and followed a good example. Perhaps their faith compels them to act. Perhaps a family member recruited them. There was likely a catalyst at first, but now they expect such responsibilities to come their way and they seek out responsibilities if there is a lull.

Accepting more responsibility does not mean doing the work which results in a front page newspaper account of your heroic effort. Most people do not live front page lives; rather, we live everyday lives. Everyday living does not mean ordinary; rather it means continuous, day-to-day, each day.

More responsibility can be accepted every day as an aging family member needs more help today than yesterday.

More responsibility can be accepted when we notice someone who needs help getting groceries to her car. More responsibility can be accepted when we ask a blind person if he needs help crossing the street.

When we make a mistake there is no need to let the mistake linger and become permanent. "That was my fault. I'll fix it." Accepting more responsibility is part of the mature response to imperfection being part of the human condition.

The most dynamic, meaningful, useful important lives are filled with more and more responsibilities. The most dynamic, meaningful, useful, important parts of life include fulfilling our responsibilities.

There is a limit. Do not accept 25 hours of responsibility for 24-hour days, but seek to fill the moments and the hours with productive rewarding responsibilities punctuated occasionally, of course, with a nap. Accepting more responsibility and taking more naps can be a great combination.

Please list new, proper, wholesome responsibilities that you could accept. You could also think of current responsibilities that could be done better.

New Responsibilities to Accept   Current Responsibilities to do
                                      Better

- •   •

- •   •

- •   •

- •   •

- •   •

93. CONTINUE MORE TRADITIONS

Family traditions are to be cherished. Continue your family traditions which began generations ago when, on Christmas morning, Bible verses were read before any packages were opened.

Continue the family tradition of volunteering time at a homeless shelter to feed people on Thanksgiving at noon and then have your family meal later.

Continue the tradition on Saturday morning of Dad fixing pancakes for Mom and the children. Continue the family tradition of everyone being home on Tuesday evening with no coming or going, rather, it is pure family time.

Continue the community tradition of celebrating the town's history each year on the day of the town's founding. Continue the community tradition of candidates for mayor appearing together many times to respond to questions presented in person by voters.

Continue the school tradition of beginning each day with recital of the pledge to the flag. Continue the school tradition of 8th graders memorizing the Gettysburg Address. Continue the school tradition of unique events designed exclusively for seniors during their final year of high school.

Continue the church tradition of singing the hymns of centuries ago so those words of wisdom and of faith endure.

Continue the church tradition of architecture which is uniquely consistent with reverence and worship.

Continue the personal tradition of taking one day per year to evaluate the past year and set goals or make plans for the next year.

Continue the tradition of keeping a diary with personal reflections.

Continue those traditions by defending more traditions from the consuming forces of technology or fast-paced living. In a high-technology world, see what happens if you write a letter and mail it via the post office. It could get noticed with greater impact than anything electronic. In an electronic world, it is still possible to walk to a neighbor's house and visit face to face.

Continue more traditions by asking older family members what traditions have faded, but could be started anew, perhaps with an innovation as needed.

Begin new traditions. For the family which is separated with different generations living in various cities, have a family conference call weekly, perhaps with video. That could be family-friendly technology.

For the business executive whose family-owned restaurant has grown to five locations, teach your managers to create time to know each employee by name as you did when you taught each employee in the original location how to do each part of every job.

For the church which must be meaningful to a generation that equates what is on a computer or cell phone screen with what is real, send supplemental follow-up electronic messages and electronic sermons, but be sure everyone is together often face-to-face. Mechanical electronics do not equal or replace personal encounters.

Traditions help give meaning, perspective, assurance and continuity. Continue more traditions and begin new traditions which a future generation will continue also.

94. ADMIT MORE MISTAKES

To myself.
To friends.
To colleagues.
To family.
To God.
To spouse.
To children.
To heritage.

The purpose of admitting mistakes is not to overstate the importance of confession. Nor is it necessary to find the person from 30 years ago who you cut line in front of at lunch in middle school to resolve that matter.

The purpose of admitting mistakes is to inventory your integrity, to confirm that you can identify what you have done that was mistaken, improper, wrong. Then, you will know what you can or should do to correct the mistakes.

First, admit more mistakes by reflecting on the categories of life that are most important yet are also most likely to have had a mistake made there. Think of family, friends, relationships, finances, career, school, community activities, church, politics and promises. What did you do very well? What was done the opposite of very well, actually in the mistake category?

Mistakes include errors made and opportunities missed. The food you could have taken to a friend after her out-patient surgery is an act of kindness that should have happened. What good you could have done and should have done, but did not do goes in the mistake category known as "What might have been."

Second, do not berate yourself for mistakes you have made. Correct mistakes if possible and practical. Apply the lessons learned from mistakes to minimize or to prevent future mistakes.

Third, some mistakes will require expert, professional help to correct. Get that guidance if it is needed.

Now, correct the mistakes. "Hi, this is Ellen Hunter. I've thought of you so many times since your accident. I should have called last week and I'm so sorry I did not, but please tell me anything I could do now that would help you and your family."

Take a few minutes right now and think of mistakes you have made. Then think of ways you could correct those mistakes. Select one mistake and begin correcting it today. Finish the correction soon.

Admit more mistakes and then correct more mistakes. Then learn from the process to reduce the number of, and seriousness of, mistakes.

95. ACCEPT MORE JOY

Life hurts. Illness creates agony. Natural disasters destroy lives and property. Accidents leave the survivors facing a life that will never be the same. Wars destroy people, property, peace. Life hurts. Starvation kills. Homelessness haunts. Job layoffs shatter dreams, communities and families.

In the midst of life's hurts, there is the possibility of joy. Where do you find joy? Beyond happiness or entertainment, beyond pleasure or amusement, to the depth of the radiant goodness within life, where do you find joy?

Once found, do you accept the joy that extends itself to you? Do you cheer for a stunning sunrise? Do you give thanks for the night sky's artistry of stars beyond number? Do you embrace the beauty of a classic symphony which touches notes of perfection? Do you marvel at the fact that people can travel continent to continent and find joy in the possibility of helping people in need thousands of miles away?

Accept more joy. Accept the gift of this day which in its presentation to us is perfect. Will our efforts extend that perfection or reverse that perfection?

Accept more joy. A family member calls you at a time when you are busy with something that seemed important, but in all honesty, can wait. Accept the joy that the conversation offers, then complete your original task with renewed vigor.

Confront and deal with the difficult realities of life knowing that life also includes, creates, longs for, and offers joy or, at least, offers opportunities for joy to be created. Seek more joy. Create more joy. Accept more joy.

Please think of the aspects of life which are truly joyous, but are underappreciated. Resolve to more fully accept those awaiting joys.

In the ordinary events of a day, are there times of under-noticed joy? "Yeah, it's a really pretty day, but I'm in a hurry, so I'll think of that later." What else in the common, daily moments can become uncommon joy when given the chance?

96. OFFER MORE HOSPITALITY

There are people who make you feel at home with your first step into their house or apartment. From the minute you enter until the minute you leave, their hospitality surrounds you. How is this done?

Perhaps those people treat their family with the same hospitality. Perhaps the culture of that family is to look out for and to take care of the needs each family member has. That culture continues daily for family members and for guests. The home atmosphere is perpetual hospitality.

It is easy to associate hospitality with food, especially with really good cooking. I never cook. Cooking and then cleaning up take time. Yogurt, an apple, a peanut butter sandwich are available instantly and have a one minute clean up time. I do know how to fix absolutely delicious homemade granola bars. My brother, sister-in-law, and their children love those granola bars. Their friends come to their home and ask, quite hopefully, for a granola bar. Sharing homemade granola bars is an act of hospitality.

Offer more hospitality. It intrigues me that the word hospitality expands the word hospital. At a hospital we hope that sick people will become well and that well people can return to their regular life renewed. Hospitality at home says to a guest you will feel better when you leave and you will return to your home refreshed.

Offering hospitality is good for the recipient and for the giver. To offer hospitality is to express your desire that other people are comfortable, cared for, and at ease. Pure hospitality overlaps with kindness, with thoughtfulness, with concern, with manners, with love.

Hospitality can be offered at work as we make our workplace more welcoming, more cordial, more congenial, more pleasant, and more humane.

The next time you attend a gathering which really impresses you because the hospitality was superior, analyze what happened and how it happened. The skills of hospitality can be learned. The heart of hospitality can be nurtured.

Please list the best examples you have seen or participated in of superior hospitality and think of how to apply those examples:

Examples of Hospitality   Apply Those Examples

- •   - •

- •   - •

- •   - •

- •   - •

- •   - •

97. LEAD MORE CHEERS

"I hope it goes well for you." That comment could apply to a friend who has a job interview, a family member who is making a presentation at work, a neighbor who will lead her church's effort to buy new property, a friend who you see in a doctor's office and who needed to be cheered up.

Lead more cheers. My experience during almost three decades as an educator shows me that most students do what they are supposed to do most of the time. For that they avoid punishment. My experience during eight years of working in advertising at three large companies is that most employees did what they were supposed to do most of the time. For that they got paid and usually avoided getting laid off. Something is missing when people work hard and do what is right only to have nothing said or done.

Lead more cheers. When good work is done, cheer about it, celebrate it, appreciate it. We get more of what we reward, of what we celebrate, of what we make a big deal about. To get students or workers to improve, cheer when good work is done.

Lead more cheers for individuals whose lives have little or no cheering, whose lives have little or nothing to cheer about. Some of your church's members cannot come to church due to health problems. Cheer them up by bringing church to them. Record the service and play it for them. Sing hymns. Read the church announcements. For people who cannot get to the activities of life, the activities of life must be brought to them.

Leading more cheers includes looking for parts of life to cheer about. Keep looking, you will find more and more to cheer about.

Leading more cheers includes looking for people who need someone to cheer for them, to cheer them up, to give them something to cheer about. Life is filled with people who have such needs and with people who need to reach out to them. Everyone will need to be cheered for or cheered up at some time. Do some cheering now for other people and life should arrange for people to cheer for you in your time of need.

Consider the questions, "Why doesn't somebody do something for them?" or "Why doesn't somebody do something about that?" Lead the cheers for action and then lead the action. Lead the cheers for other people. Don't wait for other people to begin making life better. Take action. Do something like leading more cheers.

Think of someone you know who would be thrilled if you cheered for them, if you cheered them up. Who is that person? What could you do for them today?

98. BE MORE THOUGHTFUL

Feed the hungry.

Visit the lonely.

Comfort the sad.

Encourage the discouraged.

Express appreciation for acts of kindness.

Thank a teacher, a police officer, a nurse, a firefighter, a trash collector, a childhood friend.

Seek forgiveness.

Offer forgiveness.

Donate to charities.

Be there.

Volunteer your time, talents and effort.

Call elderly friends regularly to see how they are, what they need.

Be less critical and more understanding.

Hug your spouse often, then more often than that.

Hug your children often, then more often than that.

Who could I help today?

What selfless acts of thoughtfulness could I begin today?

Who needs to hear from me today?

What do I have more than enough of that I could easily donate?

Who at school or work do I never speak to that I can and will speak to this morning?

Who did something kind for me and I still need to thank them?

To whom and in what way can I be thoughtful right now?

How can I be thoughtful right now to:

- My parent(s)/guardian(s)

- My teachers

- My brother/sister

- My neighbors

- My friends

- People who are hungry

- Homeless people

- Elderly people

- Other people

99. QUIT MORE JOBS

Despite recessions, for some people there are more jobs than they can get to in a lifetime. There are more career adventures than can fit into any one job, one workplace, one place of employment. There are jobs which provide money, jobs which provide meaning, jobs which provide money plus meaning, jobs which stretch your brain and jobs which break your heart. There is no perfect job, but some jobs are better than others.

Quitting a job is done after much reflection, thought, advice and analysis. Reality is a powerful factor to consider. Do not quit a job today and create financial difficulty or despair for yourself or your family. Some jobs must be endured, even if they are not ideal, because they serve essential ends such as income or benefits.

If the economy in general permits and if your personal economy permits, then consider leaving a job when the point of diminishing returns hits. It is wise to already have your next job secured prior to leaving your current job. Quitting more jobs does not mean to be in a fantasy world; rather, it means that, if possible, be willing to seek better or best rather than settling for good or ordinary or worse.

I will quit more jobs. I will not quit in anger or in frustration. I will quit in eager pursuit of a new adventure, a healthier work environment, more energetic and more creative colleagues, more application of my talents, more opportunities to develop new talents and more chances to touch lives.

I will quit more jobs and start insisting that my work and my life are friendly to each other. Extended time in the office is time when walks were not taken, when children were not played with, when books were not read, when exercise was not experienced, when volunteer work was not done for the community, when music was not listened to, when a sunset was not watched, when enough sleep was not gotten and when family came in second to career. Some 80-hour work weeks in the office or at the factory or in the studio or elsewhere at a job may occasionally be necessary. At those times I will arrive earlier than anyone and stay later than anyone, but the next week will be different or that is a job I need to seriously consider quitting.

I will quit more jobs if I find myself surrounded by lazy, incompetent or evil people. I will not do their job for them. I will find a place where commitment is the norm, where competence is certain and where everyone completes duties capably. Is that a dream? No, that is a requirement I place upon employers who would expect me to stay for years.

I will quit more jobs. That does not just mean I will quit my job frequently; rather, I will tell my employer when I am given particular tasks within my job that are no challenge to me yet which could be a challenge and growth opportunity for someone else. Maximize the application of my skills or I'll seek a job which does stretch me toward and beyond the current frontier of my thoughts and skills.

I will quit more jobs if I am treated unfairly, inhumanly or childishly. Inaccurate evaluations, public criticism, impossible workloads or silly political game playing will make my decision to quit very easy to reach.

I will quit more jobs because there are better jobs, but I will not quit flippantly or irresponsibly. I will not let a bad mood cause me to lose my income in an angry "I quit" demonstration. I will think and I will plan before I quit, but I will quit more jobs.

I will quit when a job becomes death-defying because I am asked to do the work load of two or three people. I will quit when the workplace is unsafe. I will quit when my employer is stuck in the past, thus limiting my current effectiveness. I will quit when my heart or soul or mind or body are made sick by my work.

I will quit more jobs and I will live more dreams and embrace more adventures and try more new ideas. I will quit more jobs, and that means I will live with work as part of my life, not with work in control of my life. I will quit jobs which are deadly because I was born to fully live.

I will quit how I think about a job. The job could be much better than I realize. Some people may love the job. Other people may seek the job. I will learn what they know about this job and rather than always quitting, although that can be necessary,

223

sometimes I will quit thinking about a job the way I was and I will quit doing a job they way I was. That is another good way to quit.

I could stay at a job and benefit from a new attitude about the job or a change in my job description. There are various ways to quit and if my thoughts are the problem, I will change them so I change my satisfaction with my current job. Then, there are other times, when quit means leave. I will learn how to tell the difference between a job attitude I must change and a job I must leave.

100. NOTICE EVEN MORE MIRACLES

A baby smiles.

A newborn horse walks.

Plants grow.

Flowers blossom.

The brain sends a message to the hand which moves in exactly the direction it was told to.

Two people, once total strangers, celebrate their 50th wedding anniversary.

Traffic lights help bring order to that which otherwise is certain chaos.

The four seasons take turns.

Students learn how to divide fractions.

Stars twinkle.

Angry people forgive each other.

A medicine is discovered, a disease is cured, a life is renewed.

A child is adopted.

Volunteers read to residents at a nursing home.

An alcoholic quits drinking.

A high school drop-out returns to school and graduates.

A church feeds the hungry.

A mortgage loan is approved.

A marriage proposal is accepted.

An apology is offered.

Traffic waits with no horns blowing as an elderly person slowly, persistently, painfully takes small steps to cross the street after the light changed for traffic to go.

Special Olympic participants are all crowned as very deserving winners.

Forgiveness is sought and is given.

A teenager who vandalized property makes total restitution.

An elderly couple holds hands.

The lights come on with the flip of a switch.

A checkbook balances.

What was lost is found.

The medical test results are negative.

Snow melts and streets are clear again.

The job interview went well.

Your call was returned.

Each anniversary is better and better.

The child who always got in trouble starts to behave.

The college degree is completed.

"I now pronounce you husband and wife."

"You are hired."

"I love you."

We are surrounded by miracles that can be noticed or ignored. Notice more miracles and absorb the endless power of the miracle of life itself.

101. SHARE MORE: A BONUS RECIPE

I know almost nothing about cooking, but I do know how to make homemade granola bars. My niece and nephews love these delicious creations from Uncle Keen's kitchen. Students through the years have celebrated the arrival of "Babbage Bars" although the increased number of young people with peanut allergies meant I had to stop bringing these treats to school. I do give the recipe to students who heard from former students about "Babbage Bars". The recipe is below.

Ingredients:
granola
peanut butter
honey
milk chocolate chips

Pour a box of 18 ounces of granola into a large mixing bowl. Pour 11.5 ounces of milk chocolate chips in the bowl. Pour a lot of honey, maybe 20 ounces, into the bowl. Put a lot of peanut butter, maybe two cups, into the bowl.

Mix everything until it all sticks together into one big ball or mound. Add more peanut butter and/or honey if everything is not sticking together.

Then put the ball of granola bar mix into a baking pan, perhaps about 13 inches by nine inches. Flatten the granola bar mixture. Cover the pan with wax paper or other covering material and put the pan in the freezer.

Later, when it is time to cut the full pan of mixture into bar size treats, put the pan in the refrigerator until it becomes soft enough to cut into small squares or rectangles. Keep the pan in the refrigerator with the treats in it or put the treats on plates to keep them refrigerated.

Here's an idea. Make a batch of "Babbage Bars". Take a walk. Read a book. Put the granola bars in the refrigerator. Take a nap. Have a treat.

Then use your favorite recipe for your favorite food item. Cook that and take a meal to a friend who is recovering from surgery or to a family which is new to your neighborhood. Share the food and share some time. This could be the start of a plan which includes share food, share time, get more exercise and take more naps. Those actions are good for you, for the people you help and for life itself. Why wait?

ACKNOWLEDGMENTS

Dr. Adron Doran and his dear wife, Mrs. Mignon Doran, were and will always be inspirations to me. I cherish the memories of their advice, their guidance, their example, their love, their faith and their integrity. They live in heaven now. I miss them.

Dr. and Mrs. Doran were neighbors of my parents in the late 1940s soon after my parents had married and settled in Lexington, Kentucky. Adron Doran was completing his doctorate at The University of Kentucky. My father had served in World War II, returned to Kentucky, and met my mother at the University of Kentucky. They were married in 1948 and a few years later my brother, Bob, and I were added to the baby boomer generation.

Dr. and Mrs. Doran were in my grandparent's generation. Much has been written about the generation which fought and won World War II; however, that generation was made who they were by the generation which reared them, taught them, guided them.

My grandparents and their contemporaries, such as Dr. and Mrs. Doran, knew right from wrong, polite from impolite, honor from dishonor, honest from dishonest, truth from deception, moral from immoral, what mattered from what was unimportant.

Dr. and Mrs. Doran served Kentucky during the many years when he was President of Morehead State University. In retirement, the Dorans were very active in their church, in the community, in the lives of former students, and in the lives of friends.

Dr. and Mrs. Doran had a wonderful Christmas Eve tradition of welcoming my mother and me to their home. My mother and Mrs. Doran would discuss cherished memories. Dr. Doran would encourage me as I completed my doctorate, wrote books, worked in school administration, and worked as a teacher.

Life in the United States would be much better if the ethics, integrity, honor, manners, work ethic, sense of duty and responsibility, faith, hope and love of Dr. Adron Doran and Mrs. Mignon Doran and their generation became the norm. It is with the deepest devotion that this book is dedicated to the Dorans and in memory of those highly honorable, exemplary people.

ABOUT THE AUTHOR

Dr. Keen J. Babbage

Dr. Keen J. Babbage has 30 years of experience as a teacher and administrator in middle school, high school, college, and graduate school. He is the author of *911: The School Administrator's Guide to Crisis Management* (1996), *Meetings for School-Based Decision Making* (1997), *High-Impact Teaching: Overcoming Student Apathy* (1998), *Extreme Teaching* (2002), *Extreme Learning* (2004), *Extreme Students* (2005), *Results-Driven Teaching: Teach So Well That Every Student Learns* (2006), *Extreme Economics* (2007, 2009), *What Only Teachers Know about Education* (2008), *Extreme Writing* (2010), *The Extreme Principle* (2010), *The Dream and Reality of Teaching* (2011), *Reform Doesn't Work* (2012), The *Power of Middle School* (2012), *Teachers Know What Works* (2013), *Can Schools Survive?* (2014) and *Life Lessons from a Dog Named Rudy* (2014). He is co-author with Laura Babbage of *Life Lessons from Cancer* (2013).

CHECK OUT THESE OTHER GREAT TITLES!

www.ingramcontent.com/pod-product-compliance
Lightning Source LLC
Chambersburg PA
CBHW031954040426
42448CB00006B/347